WHITTINGTON

WORCESTERSHIRE

A HISTORY OF
THE VILLAGE

COMPILED FOR THE MILLENNIUM
BY
LES WILTSHIRE

Front cover:
Crookbarrow Farm, Whittington (LW)

Back cover:
Whittington C of E Primary School (P&S/RJ)

Published by Whittington Village Hall
11 Berkeley Close, Whittington,
Worcester WR5 2RF

Printed by The Tudor Press (Redditch) Ltd.
Units 13-15 Howard Road,
Redditch B98 7SE

ISBN 0-9538223-0-3

INTRODUCTION

The first "History of the Village" of Whittington was produced in 1977 by Michael Craze, T.D., M.A. to mark the Silver Jubilee of Her Majesty Queen Elizabeth II. Michael updated that book in 1992, with its printing financed by the Village Hall Management Committee, whose property he intended it to be.

The village of Whittington is under pressure from the City of Worcester and its developments of Warndon to the north and St. Peter's to the south. With this and the dawning of the new Millennium in mind, it seemed a good idea to compile a new book charting the history of our village.

Using Michael's books as a base, with the blessing of his family, the intention was to expand on certain chapters adding a selection of old photographs, together with a few memories and personal recollections.

This book has been financed by a grant from the Millennium Festival Awards for All Scheme with all profits from its sale going to Whittington Village Hall. I hope that the Village Hall Management Committee will reap the benefit of this project and that the book will be read with enjoyment.

Les Wiltshire

CONTENTS

The Name and the Place

The Bounds

Domesday Book

Crookbarrow Hill

Crookbarrow Farm

Old House Farm

Church Farm

The Quartersessions

The Village Stocks and The Pound

The Whittington Gallows

Elizabeth Stephens Charity

Fanny Clifton Charity

Parish Rule before 1895

The Parish Council

Population and Census Returns

The Swan Inn

The Village Shops

Whittington Chapel and Church

The Holden Family

Rear Admiral Herbert Brace Powell

John Walker

Abraham Edward Perkins

Mrs. Henry Wood

The Chapelry

Church Lane

Walkers Lane

Royal Celebrations

The Village School

Whittington Hall

The College for the Blind

Benjamin Williams Leader RA

Berkeley Close

Woodside

Whittington and District Women's Institute

Whittington Cricket Club

Whittington and District Young People's Club

The Village Hall

The Crookbarrowers

M5 Motorway

And Finally.....

THE NAME AND THE PLACE

As well as our Whittington, there are Whittingtons in Staffordshire, Lancashire, Cambridgeshire, Gloucestershire, Shropshire and Derbyshire, all of them Saxon 'Shires'.

The name Whittington was derived from 'the enclosure (-ton) 'belonging to' (-ing) a Saxon called 'White'. In our own area are Huddington, Eckington and two Harvingtons, all similar Saxon enclosures.

The Angles and Saxons came to Britain from the North German coast in search of more land from the fifth century on, settling first in coastal areas but later travelling up the rivers. By the end of the seventh century, Worcester was the capital of a tribe called the Hwicce, whose land included parts of Wiltshire and Oxfordshire, as well as all Gloucestershire, Warwickshire and, of course, Worcestershire. They made Worcester their administrative centre long before the Bishopric was founded in 680 A.D. So Whittington must already have been 'White's enclosure' by the start of the seventh century. It had everything that a 'family' living on the land could possibly want. There was ploughland and pasture, water in the Long Brook and a natural watchtower in what they called 'the Barrow'. A Saxon 'family' included three generations of free men and women and any number of slaves, between them keeping watch day and night, fire and cattle thieving being the commonest dangers.

THE BOUNDS

A Charter of 980 A.D. in the British Museum gives the HWITINTON bounds. They begin in the southeast and go clockwise, as in most Anglo Saxon surveys. From 'TYDA'S CLEARING' the walker reaches the 'RED WAY', goes down it and then veers west of the 'BARROW' (BEORH). It is the same today, over a thousand years later. The official parish boundary still starts at the back of THE FIRS, reaches the PERSHORE ROAD, goes down it for 300 yds and then veers left behind 'CROOKBARROW HILL'.

The Saxon bounds went on to 'PLUM RIDGE' and the 'COLD SPRING' and 'REED CLEARING' (HREOD LAEGE) and 'HIGH STREET' (HAEH STRAETE), that is, the LONDON ROAD. Arthur Jones in his book 'Anglo Saxon Worcester (1958)' placed the REED CLEARING at the back of his own house, 12 Whittington Road. It would have been thereabouts but was probably more extensive than that.

These Saxon bounds went up the road to 'SWINES HEAD' (SWYNES HEAFOD), Swinesherd on the left of the Spetchley Road, and then swung right to 'CYNHILD'S HOMESTEAD', south of Swinesherd Farm. Passing through a meadow beside a wood going down a hedgerow they reached the LONG BROOK, from there they continued to 'BROAD MOOR RIDGE' and along a 'BOUNDARY DYKE' to a second 'HIGH STREET' going down this as far as the Brook, then kept above the low lying land till they crossed the HIGH STREET and from there came back to 'TYDA'S CLEARING'.

This second High Street was a Roman cart road and pack horse route and is still shown as a bridleway on the modern Ordnance Survey maps. The route travels from the junction of Berkeley Close along Brewer's Lane, passing under the motorway to Old House Farm and on to eventually meet the B4084 at Low Hill.

These Saxon bounds were probably three centuries old by 980 A.D. and remained until they were changed by the City of Worcester (Extension) Order of 1931. Whittington lost the Whittington Road, the College for the Blind and much else in that area, enabling the city to build up to Walkers Lane.

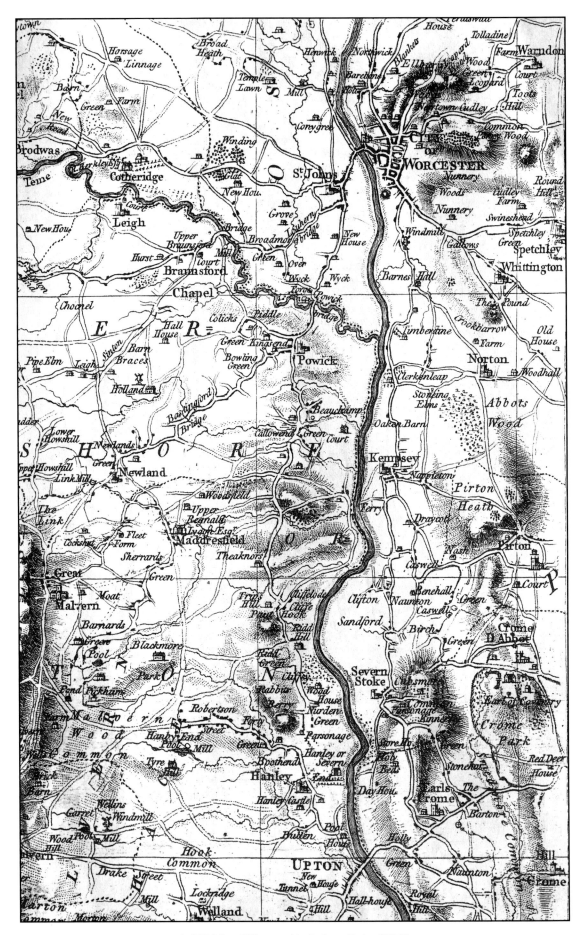

A 1772 Map of Worcestershire by Isaac Taylor (WRO)

DOMESDAY BOOK

The name Domesday Book reflects the awe with which this document was regarded. The survey was ordered by William I at a council in Gloucester at Christmas 1085, and executed with the full written report completed in the astonishingly short time of a year and nine months.

Whittington was the land of The Church of Worcester in The Oswaldslow Hundred and has two entries in the Domesday Book.

The first entry for Whittington reads: -

> *Of the same manor Walter Ponther holds 2 hides at Whittington. They were in demesne TRE; Aethelric held them in the same manner as the above hides. In demesne are 2 ploughs and 4 slaves; and 3 villans and 7 bordars with 4 ploughs, and a fishery rendering 4s., and 12 acres of meadow. (There is) woodland 1 league long and a half wide. TRE it was worth 30s.; now 40s*

The second entry for Whittington reads: -.

> *Of the same manor Walter Ponther holds 1½ hides at Whittington and 'RADLEY' (in St Peter the Great), and there he has 1 plough, and 7 bordars with 2 ploughs, and 2 slaves. There are 16 acres of meadow, (and) woodland (sufficient) only for firewood. It was worth 20s; now 25s. Aethelric held it like those above.*

The various terms used are explained as follows: -

BORDARS - a cottager, a peasant of low economic status.
SLAVES - wholly unfree, the chattels of their lord and had no land.
PLOUGH - implies a plough team of 8 oxen and the plough itself
HIDE - area of about 120 acres
MEADOW - common land for hay
LEAGUE - this term was quite common from 1066 onwards and is taken as being 12 furlongs or 1½ miles.
DEMESNE - Home farm cultivated by the labour of tenants holding lands and dwellings of the Lord.
TRE - (Tempore regis Edwardi) in the time of King Edward i.e. Before 1066 and values quoted are before and after the same date.

The area known as Radley (RODELEAH) is now lost, but may have been located somewhere in the area of the REED CLEARING mentioned in The Bounds.

It is interesting to note that evidence still exists locally of the elongated ridge and furrow form of cultivation used in medieval England.

As far as the Domesday Survey is concerned, Whittington seemed to cover a large tract of land. There is no record in Domesday of Battenhall, Barnes (Barneshall) or Timberdine so it is fair to suppose that those manors were included with Whittington for this survey, especially as it shows a fishery of some considerable value, and so probably extended to the River Severn, as Timberdine now does.

The area included in this survey is separate to, and should not be confused with, the parish boundaries set in the charter of 980 A.D.

CROOKBARROW HILL

Crookbarrow Hill or "Whittington Tump", as it is known locally, is for many people Whittington's chief claim to fame. It is used by many as a landmark when approaching Worcester from the South East, and I am sure this has been the case for centuries.

The Tump from the Motorway Junction 1964 (GM)

The Saxon Charter of 980 A.D. simply called it 'the Barrow' whilst the Red Book in 1182 referred to it as 'Cruck Hill' (CRUCHULLE). Treadway Russell Nash in his 'History of Worcestershire' in 1782 spelt it 'Cruckbarrow Hill'.

Nash wrote:

> "It consists of about six acres, of an oval form and considerable height. I cannot think it was made of earth brought here, but that the hill, being naturally irregular, was formed by art into this shape. What the use of it was is difficult to say. It is much too big for a keep to the little house or castle below.
>
> It seems too near the castle of Worcester for a watch tower, or beacon, not being much above a mile distant, and at Spetchley about three miles distant is another hill of the same kind. It seems too large for a burying mound, though it may be so called".

There is an interesting account of Crookbarrow Hill in the Transactions of the Worcestershire Naturalists Club, Volume IV, 1909-1910. This was edited by Carleton Rea and mentioning a broken flint scraper, he stated that: -

> "Much has been written respecting the origin of Crookbarrow Hill, and speculation has been rife as to its date, but, as far as I am aware, no other object has ever been found which would serve to connect it with either of the prehistoric periods".

He then writes about the Good Friday festival: -

"So long as I can remember there has always been once a year, a great concourse of Worcester people on Crookbarrow Hill, with swings, roundabouts and other accessories for merrymaking to the very great inconvenience of the occupiers of the estate in which the barrow is situated. This annual exodus of citizens occurs on Good Friday - perhaps the most sacred of all the fasts observed by the church. So firmly established is the custom, so great are the throngs of people who attend, that in spite of all the inconvenience suffered by the tenants, no opposition, so far as I know has ever been offered to the merrymaking. Now having regard to all that we know of the way in which in early Christian times pagan festivals were turned into religious rites, I do not think we should be assuming more than the facts warrant if we assume that the present merrymaking gives us the key to the origin of the barrow. Might we not suppose that in far off days a great chief had been buried, the mound raised over his remains and an annual festival held in his honour at the place of sepulture. Might we not suppose further that in order to divert the thoughts of the people into religious channels, the mound became a preaching station in Christian times, and a Calvary erected there. How otherwise are we to account for this particular day - Good Friday - being selected for merrymaking at this spot. The sequence of events therefore would be a Neolithic Burial, a pagan festival, a Christian Calvary, a modern merrymaking".

Whittington Fair 1910, presumably held in the fields near Crookbarrow Hill (WCL)

Worcestershire County Council archaeology service in their County sites and Monuments record describes it as: -

"A large elliptical mound with artificial top; its character and origin are unknown. Reputed to be sepulchral, no evidence in support of this theory. Looks more like a motte than a barrow. Apparently tumular, 512 yards in circumference. Rises 50 feet vertical height, sides slope steeply. Summit 23 paces wide at ends, 38 in middle, lies East-West, never opened".

Roman coins and a 4000-year-old flint arrowhead are among items found around this site when it was excavated by archaeologists prior to the widening of the M5 motorway in 1991. In a four week period they discovered post holes for a building, various pits containing small pieces of medieval pottery and some large ditches believed to date from prehistoric times. The project officer, Derek Hurst, said at the time,

> *"if there was a prehistoric settlement here, it is possible that Crookbarrow Hill is a huge burial mound".*

Evidence was also discovered of a village at the foot of Crookbarrow Hill, which seems to have mysteriously disappeared around 1300. By the 1400's it would seem that the site had been cleared and ploughed over. Exactly why the village might have vanished is yet another mystery - Black Death is one theory.

In 1995 during the construction of a pipeline from Strensham to Worcester a large Roman settlement stretching for some 250 metres was discovered near Crookbarrow Hill. The large area over which artefacts were found suggested a small village with houses, workshops and farm buildings. Iron working waste was evident in ditch fills, which is considered interesting, because although the Roman town at Worcester is known to have been a major iron-smelting centre, smithing evidence has rarely been found.

The distinctive shape of The Tump, topped by a single tree has been adopted as the logo of both the school and the local playgroup. However, this is only a relatively recent view, as prior to 1970 The Tump was topped by a group of elm trees, which were felled along with many others in Whittington as a result of Dutch Elm disease.

During September 1999 the BBC explored the legends and mystery which surrounds Whittington Tump for a documentary series called 'History Fix'. TV personality Rory McGrath joined forces with archaeologists from Worcestershire County Council, and a local company who provided a high-tech radar survey of the mound. The radar revealed traces of a revetment or retaining wall at the bottom of the hill and also evidence of some stonework or foundations a metre or so beneath the surface on the top of the hill.

Malcolm Atkin of the county archaeology service believes that The Tump was once used as a Roman signal station or a medieval beacon tower. In Saxon times it may have been used as a marker for estate boundaries. No evidence has so far been found to suggest it was a burial mound although many people believe that is what it was once used for. His team says it could originate from 3000 B.C. and was once a ceremonial mound of some sort. We can be fairly certain that it is at least a partly manmade structure and that it has probably been adapted over the centuries to serve several purposes. It has been calculated that if it is manmade it would have taken 1000 people a year to build.

So, the mystery continues, it seems that the more you find out about The Tump, the more questions it raises. It is hoped that English Heritage, who control the site, will support further investigations and that eventually the origins of this enigma may be established.

CROOKBARROW FARM

The seventeenth century house and dove-cote of red brick that we see today is the historic moated manor house of Whittington Manor. Part of its moat is still visible. It probably dates back to at least 1330 when Sir Edmond de Hakelute held the manor of Crookbarrow for half a Knight's fee, that is, in return for equipping and providing one cavalryman in the King's wars for 20 days in each year.

In the year 1330 John Le Mercer sold the manor of Battenhall (including Whittington) to the Priory of Worcester, which held it till the dissolution of the Monasteries in 1541. The Crown then sold it to Sir John Bourne who was Queen Elizabeth's host in August 1575 when she attended a deer hunt in Battenhall Park, which in those days extended from Battenhall to beyond The Tump.

Sir John's heir in 1577 sold the property to Sir Thomas Bromley of Holt, Lord Chancellor in 1579, and his heir sold it to the Sebrights (hence the Sebright Arms in London Road). They retained the Battenhall estate, but sold Crookbarrow and Wood Hall to the London mercer and moneylender Baptist Hicks, first Viscount Camden. On his death in 1626 Wood Hall and Crookbarrow were bought by William Stephens of Stoke Newington in Middlesex, whose family occupied both houses until 1742. William's son Randall inherited the estate and his wife Mrs. Elizabeth Stephens, dying in 1668, left money for the poor in Norton and Whittington, and it was her son Thomas who, in the late 1680's, built the present Crookbarrow house and dove-cote.

In 1742 Crookbarrow was bought by Edward Ingram of White Ladies in Worcester, and this began the partitioning of Crookbarrow Manor. Edward Ingram had two children, Anne and Richard. He gave Anne the 'Chapel House' (since called the Chapelry) and its 29 acres on her marriage to a Mr. Chambers. By the time Dr. Nash wrote his History in 1782 the Berkeleys of Spetchley had bought Old House Farm of 195 acres and Richard Ingram owned what remained. On Richard's death his son Edward inherited Parsonage Farm (now called Church Farm) of 129 acres, his other son John Richard inheriting Crookbarrow Farm. Edward also inherited the newly-built Whittington Lodge with three acres adjoining; this replaced a smaller, probably half-timbered house.

It was Richard Ingram who planted the avenue of elm trees in the long drive up to Crookbarrow Farm and on The Tump. They were stricken by elm disease and were felled in 1970; their rings numbered 182, so they dated from about 1788. When both Ingram brothers died in the 1850's the Berkeleys bought Church Farm and Crookbarrow Farm in whose ownership they remain.

Crookbarrow Farm c1909, with many more trees in evidence than there are today (P&S/EB)

OLD HOUSE FARM

Old House Farm is the property of the Berkeleys of Spetchley, the track upon which it is built is the second High Street mentioned in the Saxon bounds. What is today a bridleway was once a Roman cart road and Salt Way and formed part of a Roman road system radiating from Droitwich. Salt was the means of preserving the carcasses slaughtered every autumn, and Droitwich was the local source of salt. Old House Farm and the cottages nearby are called Ersefield on some earlier maps, and the name is still used occasionally today. It originates from the stream which the Saxons renamed the Long Brook and had previously borne the Celtic name Yrse.

Old House Farm pictured in the late 1920's (HWH)

Parts of the farmhouse are believed to have been built in the 1600's and some of the timbers used in its construction are claimed to have been second-hand then! The black and white part of the building is thought to have, at one time, been an Ale House, and that a blacksmith's shop was situated nearby. The farmhouse is built right on the boundary of the Parishes of Whittington and Norton, and it is said that the meals are cooked in Norton but eaten in Whittington, and it is to Norton Parish that it officially belongs. However, much of its land lies in Whittington and it is worthy of inclusion in this book.

John Parker was born in 1792 at Old House Farm, where he went on to become tenant farmer and Master of the Worcestershire Hunt. Hunting had been suspended between 1823 and 1825 due to a shortage of funds. With John Parker as Master, hunting resumed on October 11th 1825.

Following a dispute due to a misunderstanding regarding the date of a meet, or the drawing of coverts, between John Parker and Mr. John Somerset Russell of Powick Court (later to become Sir John Somerset Pakington and first Baron Hampton), a duel with pistols took place on Kempsey Ham on March 3rd 1827. John Palmer of Hanbury was Parker's Second and John Barnesby of Brockhampton was Second to Russell. Matthew Pierpoint, who later gave his name to the well-known Worcester street, was Surgeon in Attendance. The affair passed off without injury to either party, however, tradition has it that the bullet discharged by John Parker shot away part of the whisker of his opponent. The pair were reconciled shortly afterwards at a meeting of hounds at The Cliffey.

John Parker's whipper-in, Thomas Pitt was woken on the night of February 20th 1829 by the sound of fighting hounds. Dressed only in his nightclothes, he entered the kennel from his quarters in the loft above to calm the hounds, but instead was attacked by them. His remains were discovered the next morning by John Parker and are buried in Spetchley Churchyard.

The kennels at Old House Farm, scene of the demise of Thomas Pitt some 100 years earlier (HWH)

John Parker retired from Old House Farm in 1832 due to financial problems, he went on to earn a precarious living as a wine merchant's traveller, and about 1870 became an inmate of Powick Mental Institution, where he died on January 28th 1875 aged 82. He is buried in Powick Churchyard where a stone "erected by the subscription of a few friends" marks his final resting place.

The tenants of Old House Farm in the twentieth century have been: -

1900 - 1914	Mr. Keen	1940 - 1960	Mr. Palfry
1914 - 1918	Mr. Sims	1960 - 1987	Mr. Leighton
1918 - 1940	Mr. Sinnett	1987 - present	Mr. Pearce

Mr. J. Leighton was the longest serving tenant in the last 100 years and it was during his tenancy that the farm was badly affected by the outbreak of foot and mouth disease during 1967.

Harvest time at Old House Farm during Mr. Palfry's tenancy, probably 1950's (BH)

9

CHURCH FARM

The farmhouse and adjacent barn both date from the seventeenth century. Church Farm had been part of the Crookbarrow Manor in the ownership of The Ingram Family and was purchased by the Berkeley's in the 1850's in whose control it remains.

More recent records reveal in the early 1900's the tenancy to Church Farm was held by John Pearce Pope who came to Whittington from Berkeley in Gloucestershire, probably from another farm owned by the Berkeley's. In 1906 the tenancy was taken by his daughter Sarah Hill (nee Pope) who was married to Billy Hill and she transferred the tenancy to him. As well as farming the 129 acres at Church Farm, Billy Hill owned three traction engines, which were used for timber hauling, and in those days before combine harvesters, travelled around the local farms threshing grain on a contract basis. These engines were usually parked alongside the farm buildings at the side of Church Lane opposite the church.

In 1927 Billy Hill sold up and emigrated to New Zealand. Jack Tanner, who had been farm manager and had recently married Dorothy, Billy and Sarah's eldest daughter took over the tenancy in September 1927. Jack continued to run Church Farm in the traditional manner, which included the growing of hops. Hops had been grown at Whittington since at least 1886 when the present hop kiln was built. The hops were all dried on the premises with Jack sleeping in the kiln, waking frequently to maintain a constant heat from the open anthracite fire. This operation continued for three to four weeks, with the dried, hand picked hops being packed in 'pockets' each weighing $1\frac{1}{2}$ hundredweight. An average crop was around 30 pockets, picked from seven acres of hop yards.

Jack's two sons, John and Mick both worked on the farm, Mick was waggoners boy to Tom Salisbury, and he recalls cultivating the hop yards and drilling corn etc. using horse drawn machinery. Mick also has strong memories of milking the cows by hand and of hedge cutting in the days when a billhook was the most modern equipment available. In September 1950, a week before picking was due to start, the hop-yard was blown down during the night by severe winds. Luckily the weather during the following few days was dry and the hops were picked where they lay, therefore the crop wasn't spoiled. The damage however took around four months to repair with new posts and wires having to be erected, and all the post holes being dug by hand.

John Tanner recalls the large crops of apples grown in the orchards at Church Farm which were taken by horse and dray to Court Farm at Norton to be made into cider. Anything up to one thousand gallons could be made during September and October. The majority of this would be consumed by local men who helped out on the farm at harvest time the following year.

The ploughing, hauling etc. was in those days all done by horses, the first tractor was a Standard Fordson purchased in 1942, a second one followed in 1943 at a cost of £166. Horses were a familiar sight at Church Farm and worked alongside the tractors until the mid 1960's when Jack sold the last pair.

Following his marriage in 1959, Mick left the farm to work elsewhere, but continued to live in the village. John Tanner took the tenancy from his father Jack in September 1968, September being the end of the rent year, and the month when tenancy agreements were negotiated. John, who specialised in pigs, sheep and arable crops, continued to work Church Farm until his retirement in September 1996. A dispersal sale was held on Thursday September 19th 1996 when machinery and equipment was gathered together in the field known as The Paddock, to be auctioned. Thus ended John's tenancy and a family link spanning almost 100 years. Even in retirement, John continues to raise sheep on a few acres in Whittington, the main farm and farmhouse have returned to the control of the Berkeley family.

(Above and Left) Mick Tanner surveys the damaged Hop Yard in 1950 (JT)

Hop picking at Church Farm (RJ)

11

Jack Tanner with
'Bluebell' (MT)

John and Mick Tanner seated on the roller
with Tom Salisbury and nearest
to camera 'Gypsy' (MT)

John Tanner leading 'Boxer' with Tom Stinton moulding up potatoes on Little Bank Meadow July 20th 1962 (BPS)

A general view of the dispersal sale at Church Farm on Thursday September 19th 1996 (LW)

The 1943 Fordson Tractor awaits a new owner (LW)

THE QUARTERSESSIONS

The Court of Quartersessions was one of the chief instruments of Tudor local government. Its work was revised and defined in 1590, and the court continued to carry out these terms of reference until the Local Government Act of 1888. Sessions were held four times a year by unpaid Justices of the Peace. Their powers were extensive, including jurisdiction over nearly every crime except treason. The JP's maintained law and order in their locality, supervising the administration of national legislation and the work of the parish officers, constables, coroners, highway surveyors and overseers of the poor. By the 17th century the JP's were virtually rulers of the county.

The quartersessions' records for Whittington detail various crimes and other matters dealt with by the Justices of the Peace. An example of matters dealt with in the 1600's follows: -

> *In 1619 Thomas Davyes of Whittington stole four hens worth 16d. Seven pullets worth 11d. and one hen worth 6d. The goods of William Horne.*

> *Also in 1619, petition of Eleanor Raynolds to the Justices of the Peace praying that John Brayne of Whittington, butcher, the father of her child be ordered to breed up the said child or give her money wherewith to maintain it.*

> *An entry from 1633 reads: The highway leading from the City of Worcester to the parish of St. Peter's and thence to Whittington and from thence to Stoulton and from thence to Parshore. Aforesaid is in decay and the inhabitants of St. Peter's ought to repair the same.*

There are also several entries of indictments for assault and trespass as well as orders to keep the peace.

THE VILLAGE STOCKS AND THE POUND

The village stocks were situated next to the Swan Inn on a path called The Batter. The constable could display local mischief-makers here or impound stray cattle in the pound nearby. Pound Cottage is shown in the 1838 rate assessment as coming after Rose Cottage, but immediately before the Swan Inn. The 1732 - 1800 Parish Book records that in 1781 a payment of 4s. 9d. was made for "Expenses with a woman that stopt at Whittington Pound" and another entry in 1783 covers two payments: one guinea to a surgeon "for opening the body of William Harris for Inquest" and 5s. 8d. for "Expenses at Whittington Pound on account of the inquest".

The census return for 1841 shows that James Allen, aged 60, was residing at Pound Cottage and he gave his occupation as a cheese factor.

THE WHITTINGTON GALLOWS

A grim reminder of the past is the site of the County Gallows in the private garden of 4 Whittington Road. The choice of site arose from two factors, which have long since disappeared. Firstly the Old London Road led to the site from the Bath Road and secondly, the site was situated on several acres of common land thus no single landowner was involved. The gallows were intended to be conspicuous, with dead bodies hanging on the gibbet for weeks as a deterrent to law-breakers. The hangman had an official residence behind The Elms in Walkers Lane, namely The Hangman's Cottage.

It is innocence rather than guilt that has made the site of the gallows worth preserving. In the aftermath of The Gunpowder Plot of November 5th 1605, Father Edward Oldcorne was hung, drawn and quartered there on April 7th 1606, together with his Jesuit servant Brother Ralph Ashley. Father Oldcorne had been Chaplain at Hindlip and both were innocently implicated in The Plot. Worcester's Roman Catholic High School bears Oldcorne's name.

On August 22nd 1679, as a result of the Jesuit conspiracy against King Charles II concocted by the spurious Titus Oates, Father John Wall, Franciscan priest, was hung drawn and quartered here. Another Franciscan Priest, Father Francis Leveson would have suffered the same fate, but he died in prison in Worcester on February 11th 1680. All four martyrs were among the 243 beatified by Pope Pius XI in 1929. The Blessed John Wall was canonised as Saint John Wall on October 25th 1970 by Pope Paul VI.

The last execution at Red Hill took place on Friday July 30th 1809 when Patrick Jordan and Thomas Brady were hanged for robbing and ill treating Mr. Baly of Bromsgrove on the Bromsgrove Lickey.

This mound and tree mark the spot of the gallows (LW)

Inset - Inscription on the memorial plate situated near to the site

IN MEMORY OF BLESSED JOHN WALL O.S.F. AND OTHER PRIESTS WHO DIED FOR THE CATHOLIC FAITH IN THE COUNTY OF WORCESTER.
FOR TWELVE YEARS BLESSED JOHN WALL DISCHARGED HIS PRIESTLY DUTIES AT HARVINGTON HALL, CHADDESLEY CORBETT AND IN OTHER PARTS OF THIS COUNTY IN DAILY PERIL OF DEATH.
BORN IN 1620. HE WAS ORDAINED PRIEST IN 1645 AND WAS HANGED NEAR THIS SPOT ON THE OCTAVE DAY OF THE ASSUMPTION, AUGUST 22ND 1679
TRANSIT GLORIA MUNDI.
FIDES CATHOLICA MANET.

THIS MEMORIAL WAS ERECTED BY ELLEN RYAN FERRIS OF KINGS NORTON, WORCESTERSHIRE.

THE ELIZABETH STEPHENS CHARITY

Historically this is the oldest and probably the most interesting of the Whittington Charities.

Randall Stephens of Wood Hall was also the owner of Crookbarrow. He died in 1653 and his widow Elizabeth Stephens died in 1668, both are buried in the Chancel of Norton Church. In her will she left £100 to the poor of Norton and Whittington and ordained that it should be invested in land and settled on feoffees (trustees) and that they should distribute the revenue twice a year, on Christmas Day and Good Friday. Her executor, son Thomas Stephens, put Whittington's half share to good use by building three cottages on a third of an acre of the Manor at Swinesherd and he made the parish officers the trustees. For two centuries they managed the property, which came to be known as "The Parish Cottages". The custom grew up of distributing the revenue of £2 or so once a year on St. Thomas's Day, December 21st.

In 1877 a crisis occurred, the trustees had to spend more on repairs to the fabric than the rents were worth, but the District Auditor insisted that the amount overspent should come out of their own pockets. After three Parish Meetings it was agreed in January 1880 that the Local Board be requested to order the Guardians of the Poor of the Pershore Union to sell the cottages and pay Whittington £50 of the proceeds. This they did and the surplus stayed with the Pershore Union. Thereafter the parish officers distributed the annual interest on the £50, which in 1890 was invested in Consolidated Bank Annuities (Consols).

THE FANNY CLIFTON CHARITY

The Cliftons were Worcester Solicitors and Clerks to the Dean and Chapter. The line ended when John Hill Clifton was buried at Whittington in October 1870. Miss Fanny Clifton, his sister, lived seventeen years longer, and was the Village School's "chief benefactress" with all the children attending her funeral in January 1888. Furthermore she had been in the habit of giving away sacks of coal every Christmas time, perhaps taking a cue from the Stephens Charity the distribution again took place on St. Thomas's Day, December 21st.

Miss Clifton made a will on April 8th 1882 and in it she left £1000 "with a view to continuing to the poor Inhabitants of the Chapelry of Whittington the annual distribution of coal which I have for some years made". Her executor A.C. Hooper, was to invest the lump sum (less 10% Legacy duty) in Consolidated Bank Annuities (Consols) and to join other Trustees to himself and together they were to spend the net income each year on 'coal or fuel' and distribute this at their discretion every St. Thomas's Day.

The Minute Book of this charity makes interesting reading and documents the changing winter prices of coal. In 1889 the South Wales and Cannock Chase Coal Company supplied coal at 17/- per ton delivered to Spetchley Station, and 5cwt each was distributed to 64 addresses within the Chapelry of Whittington. One can assume that the winter of 1898/99 must have been a bad one, for an extra distribution was ordered on March 24th 1899 for delivery to the same households that received supplies the previous December, the price paid was 17s. 6d. per ton. December 1914 saw coal at 24s. per ton whilst due to the shortage of labour owing to the war, by December 1918 it had risen to 43s. per ton.

A minute dated November 28th 1939 details the price at 35s. per ton and states that due to wartime restrictions the Charity had to be registered with the Cannock Chase Coal Company for the supply of coal. By December 7th 1940 the price was 41s. 3d. per ton, but the next entry in the Minute Book is not until May 8th 1946 and states that the coal ordered in 1940 was never delivered! Further supplies were ordered, however the entry for April 26th 1949 shows that this was never delivered either. It was resolved that in future coal tickets would be issued for the recipients to redeem with the coal merchants with which they were registered. With coal being used less, people being better off, and the ravages of inflation taking its toll, the sums that could be issued would amount to very little. The Charity is controlled by the Charity Commissioners in strict accordance with the original terms therefore it can only be used for the purchase of coal, and no cash payments can be made.

These Charities like countless other Victorian investments have lain dormant for several years, but remain in the control of four local trustees.

PARISH RULE BEFORE 1895

In early Victorian England the Elizabethan form of the local government was only just beginning to end, things having not changed much since the Poor Law Act of 1592. Parishes were still self-governing and self-financing and fixed their own rates. The administrative year still began and ended on Lady Day, March 25th.

The parish priest was meant to dominate the community, once appointed he could stay for life. Since 1538 he had been required to keep registers of every Baptism, Marriage and Burial. To assist him was a paid Parish Clerk and a Sexton who was generally a grave-digger and only part-time. The other parish officers: the churchwardens; the overseers of the poor; the waywarden and the constable were all elected annually, usually at Easter.

The constable was responsible for law and order within the parish bounds and had the power to arrest. In the 1830's professional policemen began to take over from the unpaid parish constable, however in 1844 the Whittington 'Vestry' appointed five men to share the office, while in 1859 the 'Vestry' returned four men as "qualified and liable to serve as constables"; one was a newspaper editor, William George of The Cottage.

The Overseers of the Poor collected the poor rate, in 1836-7 they collected a rate of sixpence (6d.) in the pound, which yielded £110. That was the first full year of the Pershore Union Workhouse, set up under the 1834 Poor Law Amendment Act, and £30 of the poor rate was sent to Pershore. For the rest of the century all hopeless cases went there. From this £110 they made weekly payments of between 6d. and 2s. 6d. to four poor widows. They paid two doctors £7 for attending the penniless at cut prices. £1 was paid for a coffin and they subsidised the mothers of two illegitimate babies, but clawed back £7 from the fathers.

The waywarden had been responsible for the upkeep of the highways and byeways until the early nineteenth century, when the highways became the responsibility of the Chapel Warden as Surveyor of the Kings Highways. (In 1839 the byeways were measured and found to be: Footpaths 2 miles 2 furlongs; Bye-roads 1 mile 264 yards). John Hampton, Chapel Warden from 1813 to 1815, had two very difficult years. The constant carting of building stone along the Spetchley Road for Squire Berkeley's new house in 1811-12 had ruined the road. Whittington was legally responsible for its repair and the county authorities threatened an Indictment at the next Assizes. In January 1813 a Vestry Meeting was called and it resolved that the road "be permanently and substantially repaired with all convenient speed ...... beginning at the Cross and Hands on Red Hill near the site of the gallows ..... and ending at the second lake or farther end of the Swinesherd Green". Between February 3rd 1813 and September 27th 1814 John Hampton had to levy £280 which represented a rate of 6s. 6d. in the pound. In the next twelve months he had to levy a further £30 to put 300 tons of gravel on "the Kings Highway from the Cross and Hands on Red Hill to Pershore as far as Mr. Palmer's brick kiln"; presumably this was somewhere near the site of The Firs.

Whittington's two "Kings Highways" were subject to the Turnpike Trustees. A rate of 1s. in the pound being paid to the magistrate in 1839 and on the 1842 Tithe Map, both are marked 'Turnpike Roads' however there were no toll-gates in Whittington. In 1865-66 the Turnpike Trustees were abolished under the 1864 Highways Act and the new Upton Snodsbury Highway Board administered our two roads. This was unpopular and in 1893 the Whittington Vestry with undisguised and long pent-up fury called on the Board to make a footpath from the main road to the church "seeing that we have but 1¼ miles of road for which we are called to pay £126 per year to the Upton Snodsbury Highway Board". A highway it was not, but they got it!

THE PARISH COUNCIL

The County Franchise Act of 1884 had increased the number of Parliamentary Electors from around three million to five million by adding all households paying a rent of £10 or more. The County Council Act of 1888 transferred to elected County Councils' powers over roads and health and much else, which until then county magistrates had administered. Rural District Councils were set up next, followed in 1894 by Parish Councils. These took over civil powers from, in Whittington's case the Chapel Warden. A Parish Meeting on December 4th 1894 elected the first seven councillors, their Chairman, two Overseers of the Poor, a Treasurer and a Clerk. It took over responsibility for rights of way, stiles and bridle paths.

Whittington Parish Council still has seven elected members plus a paid clerk, and in consultation with Wychavon District Council and Worcestershire County Council has input into highways, local planning and environmental matters.

The Chairmen of the Parish Council have been: -

1894 - 1897	S.B. Garrard	1977 - 1983	T.R. Gaylor
1897 - 1898	George Pitcher	1983 - 1995	Albert Morris
1898 - 1930	Edwin Watson	1995 - 1996	Michael Brown
1930 - 1936	Herbert March	1996 - 1998	Barrie Redding
1936 - 1940	George Pitcher	1998 - 1999	Michael Brown
1940 - 1959	J.C. Baker	May - Sep 99	Barrie Redding
1959 - 1977	R.C. March	Sep 99 Present	Roger Phillips

POPULATION AND CENSUS RETURNS

The population figures for the period 1801 to 1901 give a clear indication of the way in which Whittington grew during this era. The census returns for 1841 to 1881 give a breakdown of male and female occupants and show how many houses were inhabited.

1801		Total 105
1811		Total 169
1821		Total 207
1831		Total 279
1841	... 144 Males .... 138 Females .... 59 inhabited houses	Total 282
1851	... 143 Males .... 146 Females .... 71 inhabited houses 1 uninhabited house	Total 289
1861	... 143 Males .... 166 Females .... 75 inhabited houses 2 uninhabited houses	Total 309
	(One of the Males was living in a barn!)	
1871	... 186 Males .... 187 Females .... 85 inhabited houses 1 uninhabited house	Total 373
1881	... 179 Males .... 194 Females .... 83 inhabited houses 3 uninhabited houses	Total 373
1891		Total 401
1901		Total 384
1991		Total 337
1999	... From Electoral Register (adult voters)	Total 434

With the exception of 1999, these numbers are all total population, including children, and show that around 1800 Whittington was by any standards a very small settlement.

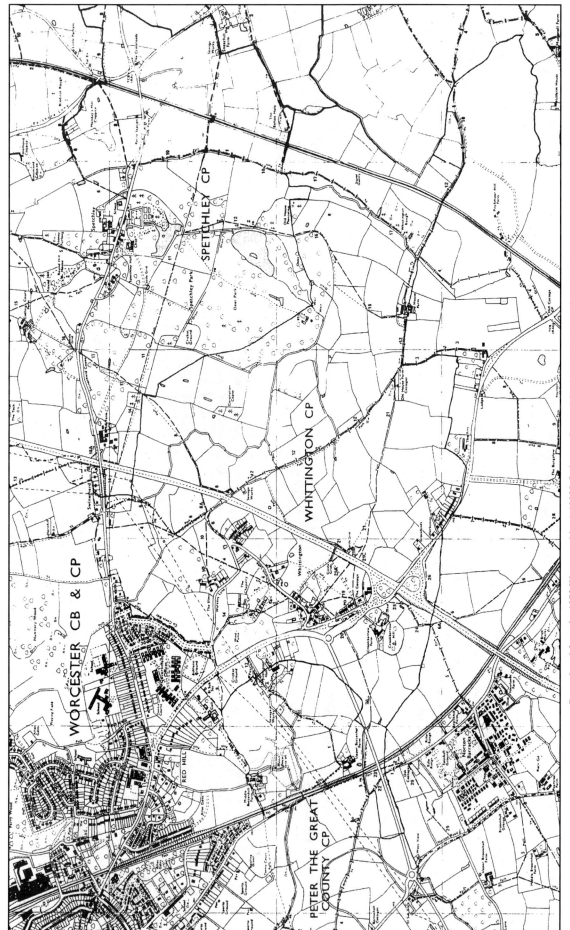

THE SWAN INN

The new Rate Assessment on February 14th 1838 details that the Swan Inn was occupied and owned by James Lane, and that the site measured 1 Acre 0 Roods 30 Perches (5747 ½ square yards). Its gross rentable value was adjudged to be £40. Allowing 15% off for repairs, its net rentable value was £34; and that was what counted for payment of rates at whatever pence in the pound. James Lane took the minutes of Parish Meetings held in The Swan.

The Swan owner at the end of the nineteenth century was an Upton Snodsbury farmer named John Hughes. He had been one of the forty scholars in the Kings School from 1866 to 1869, when he died in 1917 he left The Swan to the Kings School to found the John Hughes Scholarship for students studying Classics at Oxford. He made the Mayor, Aldermen and Citizens of Worcester trustees empowering them to sell The Swan and invest the proceeds. This they did in 1921, investing the sum of £1,150. The first holder of the John Hughes Scholarship at Hertford College, Oxford from 1925 - 1929 was Michael Romilly Craze; this scholarship is still in existence today.

The present building dates from about 1780 and occupies an ideal site on the crest of a small hill. Such a site would not have stayed vacant until 1780 and probably replaced an earlier, half-timbered building.

The census returns give a 'snap-shot' of the landlords of The Swan Inn during the late 1800's, with a selection of references from Kelly's Trade Directories giving some details for the early 1900's.

	Name	Age	Occupation
1841	James Lane	55	Publican
1851	Mary Lane	69	Vitualer
1861	Henry Harber	26	Inn Keeper
1871	Walter Weston	40	Inn Keeper
1881	Charles A Wilkins	39	Inn Keeper
1900	Thomas Alfred Wormington		
1922	James Henry Spilsbury		
1932	George Davis		
1933	Edwin Davis		
1940	Roland Price		

This is by no means a comprehensive list of landlords, but it does give a glimpse of past innkeepers.

The Kelly's directory for 1860 confirms Henry Harber as landlord of The Swan and interestingly lists Robert Page as landlord of The Star at Swinesherd, no location for this hostelry is given.

A close-up of the group at The Swan Inn with the landlord's name, Frederick Gossage, visible above the door (EB)

The Swan Inn - 1906 (EB)

The Swan Inn - 1908 (P&S/UW)

21

Swan Darts Team - Early 1940's (WP)

The Swan Inn probably 1930's (JL)

The Swan Inn photographed in 1941, complete with sign requesting travellers to "STOP AT THE SWAN THE INN THAT IS COMFORTABLE" (WRO)

THE VILLAGE SHOPS

The history of the shops in the village is somewhat hazy. The earliest record found is an entry in the 1850 Slater's directory listing Joseph Griffith as a shopkeeper. Littlebury's Directory of 1873 quotes Mrs. Ellen Birt and Elizabeth Hartland as shopkeepers and George Ewins as a boot and shoemaker, the 1881 Census shows that Mary Ann Allard, then aged 30, was postmistress, unfortunately no location for the Post Office is given. The Kelly's directory of 1884 states Miss Allard was a shopkeeper and postmistress and the Kelly's of 1896 gives Miss Allard as a shopkeeper and William Henry Ewins as sub postmaster. The 1905 Littlebury's and 1912 Kelly's directories both quote William Henry Ewins as a boot and shoe maker and sub postmaster, his business was situated at No. 1 Hill View.

Whittington and Norton Postmen c1920
The two postmen would meet each day in the field known as the Forty Acres, which is opposite
the houses in Pershore Road, where they would exchange mail for the two villages (RJ)

A village shop owned by Mrs. Kath Curnock, apparently was run from a small wooden building at the back of Maple Cottage. This site was also home to Woodware Joinery and Maintenance Co, a woodworking company run by Denis Curnock, which during the early 1950's, shared premises with Alf Brown who ran a motor repair business there. This now quiet cul de sac was then the main A44 with much passing trade for the village stores. Another shop was located at Primrose Cottage where Mr. and Mrs. Wells kept a Post Office, the Kelly's directories of 1933 and 1940 both say, "William Fredk. Wells. Shopkeeper and Post Office".

It would appear that the Post Office closed around 1947, as a letter from the Postmaster of Worcester dated April 16th 1947 was discussed at a Parish Council Meeting on April 24th, at which the council agreed to the erection of a letter box in a brick pier adjacent to the telephone kiosk opposite the Swan Inn. The council requested that a stamp vending machine be included. On February 10th 1955 the Parish Council discussed the stamp vending machine and concluded that they had no objection to its removal as it was seldom refilled, but felt the provision of a Post Office in the village was essential.

By this time Alf Brown and his wife Amy were running the village stores from the rear of their house which was just a few doors Pershore side of its previous location at Primrose Cottage. He was approached by the Parish Council with a view to taking on the Post Office; but declined. In 1958 Alf and Amy Brown sold the shop and re-located the motor repair business to Egdon Service Station.

Denis Curnock seated outside his wife's village stores. Late 1930's (JB)

The shop was taken over by Mr. and Mrs. Bourne who also took on the Post Office. The Village Stores remained here until its closure in the mid 1960's. During the period of the motorway construction Mr. and Mrs. Bourne obviously did a brisk trade, as did the local children, who collected up all the empty pop bottles left by the workmen and returned them to the shop, not forgetting to collect the deposit. Although the motorway was responsible for good business during the years of construction, it was ultimately responsible for the demise of the village stores. Once the motorway and the new dual carriageway were opened, the shop had no passing trade and even with the Post Office, had insufficient custom to keep it open.

As well as the shops detailed here, apparently other shops existed in the village. One was a tobacconist and sweet shop situated in the half-timbered cottages which once stood in School Walk and another traded in Church Terrace. The Kelly's directory of 1922 details a shop owned by Mrs. Mary Gurney which traded in Narrow Walk.

The woodworking business of Denis Curnock continued to trade at Maple Cottage, where he hand-built caravans. These caravans were sited at Newton Point, Porthcawl and let as holiday homes. I, like other local people can remember spending happy seaside holidays in one of "Den's 'vans". Unfortunately, disaster struck at the workshop, when a fire broke out one November night in 1966. The fire completely destroyed the premises, and also burned a van owned by people next door! The site was cleared and a new concrete building replaced the badly damaged wooden structure. That building stood until mid-1999, when it was demolished to make way for a residential development.

Denis Curnock's
workshop destroyed
by fire in November
1966 (JB)

WHITTINGTON CHAPEL AND CHURCH

The existence of a Church at Whittington in A.D. 816 is proved by a charter in which the King of the Mercians granted Worcester's Bishop Deneberht and his cathedral clergy exemption "from all but the three common dues and the King's food-rent at Hwitingtun".

By the sixteenth century Whittington was a Chapel of St. Peter's, Worcester under Richard Davies who was vicar of St. Peter's from 1524 to his death in 1556. In 1552 it was he and his Chapel Wardens John Staunton and William Staunton who obeyed the new Protestant Government and, in common with every church in the land, returned an Inventory of Church Goods. They said that Whittington had:

> *"A chalice and paten, silver outside but gold inside. Three vestments (one of damask, one of white fustian, one of white crewel) and two albs. A cope of green crewel. A surplice. A censer of brass. A copper cross. A pyx of latten. Two little bells hanging in the church wall".*

The paten and chalice were taken. The silver ones that have survived are hallmarked 1570 and 1571.

Thomas Habington of Hindlip (1560-1647), a godson of Queen Elizabeth I, was preparing his survey of Worcestershire in the 1630's when he left us a glimpse of the interior of the Church of that time.

> *"Whitington, a chappell attending St. Peter's Church, a mile distant from Worcester, hath no armes or funeralls, but in the east wyndowe presenteth a preyst, who by his habyte and style should be a reader in scholes, being written Magistri Ricardi, the rest broken out. And in the north wyndowe of the body of the chappell is wel peynted in the glasse a religious man prayinge, his clothing inwardly whyte and his outward habyte darke".*

The surviving registers date from 1653 when Henrie Stanton and Elinor Pinnock were married on May 2nd. The vicars and curates were ever changing, with a couple of notable exceptions. In 1753 George Boulter, who was vicar of Kempsey and also responsible for Norton Chapelry and Stoulton, came to an arrangement with Daniel Brooker of St. Peter's to go halves on the pay and employment of Richard Turner, his curate at Norton. For the next 29 years Richard Turner served 'Whittington with Norton'. The other stalwart of the same period was William Hughes, vicar of St. Peter's from 1757-85, he was apparently a merry man who took most of the Whittington weddings.

Whittington Church 1784 from a watercolour by Burney (WRO)

The great yew tree, north of the church, goes back even further. Experts date yew trees by measuring their girth a yard or so above ground level. Worcester's expert Carleton Rea measured this one on December 23rd 1932 and reported to Herbert March that it was 13ft. 7ins. round. The average yew trunk adds a quarter of an inch a year to its girth, it therefore took root here in about 1280, north of an older previous church. Yews are poisonous to cattle, but were essential for the bows of the yeoman of England in the King's Wars. By an Act of Parliament in 1466 every Englishman in every parish had to own a bow made of yew, ash or hazel and had to practice archery at the parish butts once every Church Feast Day or pay a fine of a half-penny. The range could be up to 400 yards and many places still have areas called Butts - Worcester is no exception.

Anglican church-going reached its height in the 1840's onward with the Church of England rebuilding over 7000 old chapels and churches between 1840 and 1876. Whittington Chapel was rebuilt in 1844, under the supervision of Rev. George Lardner Foxton, who came to St. Peter's with Whittington in 1840, and Chapel Warden John Walker.

Whittington Chapel near Worcester 1842 from a sketch by Nellie Hooper signed by her and dated 1862. This drawing was spotted by Canon H.B. Southwell in a Sidbury antique shop window in 1920 and given by him to Whittington Church (RPJ)

The Registers tell that on July 10th 1842 the vicar married William New and Mary Evans in the old church. On July 21st the wedding of John Barnett and Susannah Watkins was transferred to St. Peter's, "the chapel of Whittington having been taken down in order that it might be rebuilt". On Monday July 25th, St. James's Day, the corner stone of the new chapel was laid by the Rev. William Rose Holden, Chaplain of St. Oswald's Hospital in the Tything. Shortly after twelve o'clock, the procession led by the clerk of St. Peter's preceded by Mr. Perkins, the architect, Rev. G.L. Foxton, vicar of St. Peter's, the Rev. W.R. Holden and other members of the clergy "and a numerous train of the most respectable inhabitants of the parish of St Peter's and the Chapelry of Whittington" proceeded in order from the residence of the Misses Probyn to the churchyard; and "the preliminary arrangements being complete, the proceedings of the day at once commenced by the Rev. W. Holden reading a portion of the 102nd psalm". The Rev. W.R. Holden then proceeded to lay the foundation stone dedicating the chapel to St. Philip and St. James. When the ceremony was completed Hyla Holden Esq. read the inscription upon the plate as follows: -

**IN THE NAME OF
THE FATHER AND OF THE SON AND OF THE HOLY GHOST
THIS CORNER STONE OF A CHAPEL
DESIGNED FOR THE GLORY OF
THE HOLY UNDIVIDED
COEQUAL AND COETERNAL TRINITY
DEDICATED IN HONOUR OF
ST. PHILIP AND ST. JAMES APOSTLES AND MARTYRS
AND ERECTED ON THE SITE AND IN THE PLACE OF
THE ANTIENT CHAPEL LATELY STANDING
IN THE CHAPELRY OF WHITTINGTON
WAS LAID BY
WILLIAM ROSE HOLDEN CLK.M.A.
CHAPLAIN OF THE HOSPITAL OF
ST. OSWALD IN THE ADJOINING BOROUGH OF WORCESTER
ON THE FEAST OF ST. JAMES
IN THE YEAR OF OUR LORD MDCCCXLII
GEORGE LARDNER FOXTON CLK. M.A. VICAR
JOHN WALKER CHAPELWARDEN
EDWARD PERKINS ARCHITECT
OTHER FOUNDATION CAN NO MAN LAY THAN THAT IS LAID
WHICH IS JESUS CHRIST**

Several newly struck silver and copper coins including a shilling and a half farthing dated 1842 were afterwards placed in a bottle deposited in the stone, and the plate soldered down. The large silver trowel used on the occasion was specially made by Mr. Skarratt of Worcester, at a cost of £5.13s., and bore the following inscription: -

"Presented to the Rev. William Rose Holden, M.A., on the occasion of his laying the first stone of the new Chapel at Whittington, July 25th 1842.

*Rev. G.L. Foxton, M.A. Vicar
John Walker Esq. Chapelwarden
Edward A. Perkins Esq. Architect."*

Following the ceremony the company retired to Walkers Place, the home of John Walker the Chapel warden, where a veritable feast was enjoyed by all. The celebrations continued well into the evening and all classes were wined and dined, with entertainment from the chapel choir, whilst labourers engaged on the church were supplied with a similar feast at the Swan Inn. Berrows Worcester Journal of July 28th 1842 gave details of the design.

"It will be built in the early English style of architecture, with four lancet windows on each side, a south porch, and a bell turret at the west end, a well proportioned Chancel 16ft. by 12 ft. 6 ins., lighted by a triple lance window. The outside will be of blue lias stone raised on the estate of Benjamin Hooke, Esquire, of Norton and hammer dressed in a manner happily appropriate for a village church. The upper stage of the bell turret, cappings, cornices, string courses, windows etc. will be of stone from Elmley Lovett quarries".

After the demolition of the old building, the great yew tree, now suddenly visible to all, was giving cause for concern. The tree was already hollowing and its limbs were parting above the trunk. In an effort to save the tree, an iron collar was fitted around its two principal limbs.

An entry in the Chapel Warden's accounts dated April 8th 1843 states:

> *To W. Checketts ½ a day in assisting*
> *to cramp the Yew Tree*   *1s. 3d.*
> *Paint for ditto*   *0s. 6d.*

A century and a half later the Cramp is still there, in places the yew has grown over its iron collar, and the sixpenny paint has flaked away!

The new building took twenty months to complete and on Tuesday March 19th 1844 it was consecrated by Dr. Pepys, Bishop of Worcester. He, together with some thirty clergy robed in Whittington Lodge and in bright sunshine, at 11.00am processed the few yards to the church porch for the legal formalities. The Worcester Herald reported there were "upwards of 350 people present, principally consisting of elegantly dressed ladies". In his sermon the Bishop referred to Whittington as "a poor village", saying the object of the new church was that proper accommodation and opportunity might be given to the poor to hear the word of God. The total cost of the new church was about £1,100, but the committee were still some £280 short of their goal. The Bishop urged all those present to give and the collection that followed the sermon raised £91.16s.6d.

The Church contained 247 sittings of which 139 were free. The gallery was not built for an organ or musicians, but to provide free seats, and grants of £75 from the Incorporated Society and £100 from the Worcester Diocesan Church Building Society were given dependant on half the seats being free. The inhabitants of Whittington had collected £480 and £80 was raised from the sale of materials from the old Church. The new low-backed pews could be rented or reserved. The Worcester Herald reported that following the service Miss Susan and Miss Charlotte Probyn entertained the clergy to lunch and sent every inhabitant of the village 1lb of beef, to which the vicar added 'a half-quarter loaf' (2lbs.) The Corn Laws had not yet been repealed and bread was incredibly expensive. The Census of 1841 states that there were 59 houses and 282 people in the parish.

The 1844 church had been built without any 'office and robing-room' so in 1890 Mr. Waldegrave Stone provided one. The minutes of a meeting held on April 3rd 1891 say: -

> *"Mr. Garrard proposed and the Revd. R. Relton seconded and it was carried unanimously that thanks be given to Mr. J. Waldegrave Stone for his valuable and munificent gift of a Vestry to the Church".*

An inscription on the Lych gate reminds us that it was erected "In memory of Parishioners and other Worshippers in this Church who served in the Great War 1914 - 1918", and a tablet on the north wall of the nave records the names of those who lost their lives in the First World War.

> "In grateful memory of the following Parishioners who laid down their
> lives for their country in the Great War 1914 - 1918
>
> | | |
> |---|---|
> | Private | Rupert Henry Crowther |
> | Private | Thomas Henry Dorrell |
> | Private | Walter Henry Hughes |
> | Private | Lawrence William Jones |
> | Private | Harry Ledbury |
> | Major | Charles Davies Vaughan D.S.O. |
>
> All these were honoured in their generation, and were a glory in their day"

In the Second World War, Whittington appears more fortunate than many villages, in that no parishioners lost their lives as a direct result of this conflict.

The Victoria History of Worcestershire states that the chapel at Whittington was originally held by the Church of St. Helen in Worcester. It seems that towards the end of the 15th century Whittington was transferred to St. Peter's parish, where it remained until 1910, when it was annexed to the new parish of St. Martin's.

In 1957 a new parish of Norton-with-Whittington was formed, these two rural parishes having similar requirements. The fashion for joining parishes in groups or teams encouraged the setting up in 1981 of a Worcester Team with St. Martin's, St. Mark's in the Cherry Orchard and Norton-with-Whittington. In 1986 Holy Trinity and St. Matthew, Ronkswood joined the Team, and Norton left it. At the same time Whittington's Chapelry became a second parish church in the parish of St. Martin with St. Peter, now having two churchwardens.

Since 1800 our Chapel Wardens have been:

1800 - 05	Joseph Moule	1893 - 98	H.W. Wallis
1805 - 10	John Hartwright	1899 - 1931	Edwin Watson
1810 - 11	John Winnall	1931 - 35	Herbert March
1811 - 13	William Lawrence	1935 - 56	R.C. March
1813 - 15	John Hampton	1956 - 57	Herbert Clarke
1815 - 16	Thomas Wheeler	1957 - 60	Joan Baker
1817 - 19	Thomas Silvester	1960 - 69	R.C. March
1819 - 31	John Hampton	1969 - 79	H.C. Gammon
1831 - 63	John Walker	1979 - 87	Michael Craze
1863 - 71	William George	1987 - 88	Michael Craze/Eileen Hayes
1871 - 74	Daniel Eaton	1988 - 92	Eileen Hayes/Jeffrey Eaves
1874 - 89	George Groves	1992 - 96	Eileen Hayes
1889 - 92	S. B . Garrard		Rosalind Prokopiw
1892 - 93	J. E. A. Arnold	1996 - present	David Chestney
			Peter Wheatley

During the period 1939 - 1945 Dr. Moore Ede deputised for Mr. R.C. March who was on service in the Merchant Navy.

Jim Parker was a faithful servant of Whittington Church for 67 years, born on October 23rd 1881 Jim became a bellringer in 1894 and a sidesman in 1901. By 1909 he had taken the position of clerk and verger which he continued to do until 1961. Jim passed away on September 20th 1966 aged 84; his ashes were interred in their family grave at Whittington.

It is not possible to produce a complete list of vicars, because until comparatively recently Whittington was a chapelry to the various churches mentioned and services would have been conducted by the incumbents of those churches or by their curates.

Whittington Church c1909, showing the stone ha-ha wall complete with iron railing (P&S/EB)

Whittington Church c1909. This photograph shows the chimney pipe, which according to a note in the Church records dated August 1932, belonged to "the objectionable old furnace which stood in the aisle and was quite ineffective for heating purposes" (P&S/EB)

Whittington Church c1916 (WWH/EB)

Interior view of the Church c1916, showing the pews at the front running length-ways to form choir stalls, and oil lamps clearly in evidence (WWH/EB)

Whittington Church c1916 (WWH/EB)

Interior views of Whittington Church, prior to the reordering in 1997 (LW)

REORDERING OF WHITTINGTON CHURCH

Plans for the reordering and refurbishment of the interior of the Church were first displayed to the public at a meeting at the Village Hall on September 23rd 1996.

The first phase of the scheme involved the complete re-wiring of the building, the installation of spotlights in the sanctuary and new lights in the nave and under the gallery. The heating system was renewed with all pews having heaters fitted beneath them. At the same time, a sound system and an induction loop were installed, enabling those with hearing difficulties to take greater part in the services. The church had to be closed for several weeks while this work took place, with normal services being conducted at the Village Hall during November 1996.

The second phase involved the removal of some of the pews, opening up the head of the main seating area, removing the priest's stall from the pulpit, extending the steps and moving the altar and altar rail forward. At the back, the medieval font was moved forward, some pews removed and a new bookcase and storage area installed inside the main door, thus freeing the back pew for seating and improving access for wheel-chairs and prams. The area under the gallery where pews were removed was carpeted, providing an ideal setting for meetings and a suitable space for children.

These changes have made the use of the church more flexible and more suited to modern needs whilst retaining its essential character.

Much research was carried out before the altar was moved and the floor tiles were found to have been made in Worcester by Worcester Royal Porcelain and supplied on an invoice dated January 7th 1844. The area under the stone Altar was strengthened to provide a sound foundation and during this operation the outer vault of Herbert Brace Powell was uncovered, it was photographed and reinstated.

These works took place during April, May and June 1997, with the Village Hall again being used as a temporary 'Church' when necessary. The Church finally reopened on Sunday July 6th after the final phase of work, the redecoration, was completed. The cost of the project was some £37,000.

Workmen engaged in the careful moving of the altar (PJW)

THE CHURCHYARD EXTENSION

Whittington Church is fortunate to have a Churchyard where burials may take place; Whittington is the only Church in the Worcester South East Team to have one. Space within the Churchyard was being progressively used up, the Parochial Church Council were obviously aware of the situation and had been seeking ways of overcoming the problem.

The Weston family, who had lived in the village, and farmed the Crookbarrow estate, owned the land adjoining the Churchyard. In 1995 they generously agreed to donate an area of land to provide an extension to the Churchyard. A boundary fence was erected around the extension in the summer of 1996, and early in 1997 a hedge was planted alongside and within the fence. It consisted of: - 10 Oak Trees, 200 Hawthorn, 50 Field Maple, 50 Elder, 100 Hazels. This composition of plants should enable a dense rural hedge to develop in about ten years, giving the Churchyard a sound and appropriate boundary. Both the fence and hedge were paid for by the Parish Council who are the Burial Authority. Further trees have been added including two specimen Oaks, Sycamores and Birch. A Glastonbury Thorn was planted by Whittington Women's Institute to commemorate the centenary of the national movement.

The old boundary to the Churchyard was formed by a "ha-ha", a stone wall on one side of a ditch. The unwanted growth and brambles were removed, to reveal the wall which will eventually be restored, access to the extension will be via an earth bank over the ditch.

A Service of Thanksgiving and Consecration of the Churchyard Extension was conducted on Sunday December 7th 1997 by the Bishop of Dudley, Rt. Rev. Dr. Rupert Hoare. Some 80 people gathered under ever darkening skies to give thanks for the transformation of the Church, and to witness the Consecration of the Churchyard extension. Following the service the congregation retired to the Village Hall for light refreshments.

David Chestney and Peter Wheatley (churchwardens) with Canon Michael Lewis,
Rt. Rev. Dr. Rupert Hoare and Mrs. Weston attending the consecration ceremony (DC)

Records show that the Churchyard has already been extended three times before. Firstly in 1844 just after the present Church was built. It was extended again in 1885 when land was provided by Benjamin Williams Leader and once more in 1925 with land provided by Herbert March.

THE HOLDEN FAMILY

The Rev. William Rose Holden and his wife Betty came to Worcester in 1829 when he was appointed as Chaplain of St. Oswalds Hospital. He came from the rectory of Burton Bradstock on the Dorset coast where he and his wife had raised three sons and a daughter; John, William, Hyla and Eliza.

When his second son William was ordained in 1836 he became assistant chaplain, moving into the Chaplain's house in the Tything. William Snr. and Betty moved to a newly built family house on Lark Hill, which they called Dorset Cottage.

Sadly in 1837 Betty Holden died at the age of 57 and was buried at Whittington, this was to be the first of many family burials at Whittington. In January 1842 William Jnr's infant twins Hyla and Reuben aged just three and four days were buried here by their grandfather. In July of that same year Rev. William Rose Holden laid the corner stone of the new church, to which he had been the biggest subscriber. He was the Bishop's Chaplain at the dedication service in 1844 and his son Hyla, a solicitor, gave a silver alms dish, the inscription on the reverse of which records this and other items given by him: -

> *"Hyla Holden Gent. Gave this Alms Bason together with the Flagon, Chalice and Paten to The Chapelry of Whittington on Tuesday the nineteenth day of March in the year of our Lord 1844 being the day of the Consecration of the New Chapel".*

All these items are still in use today.

On February 24th 1845 the second son Rev. William Holden was buried at Whittington, aged 32. Four years later, on March 12th 1849 Eliza Mary Holden was laid to rest at Whittington, aged 30. In 1850 the remaining family gave the beautiful east window, which was made in Newcastle upon Tyne, and dedicated as a memorial window in May that year. The glass was designed by Frederick Preedy and can be compared with the Queen Adelaide memorial window in the south transept of Worcester Cathedral, which he worked on a year or two later.

Rev. William Rose Holden was buried at Whittington on April 21st 1854 aged 78, the little north chancel window is inscribed to his memory. The eldest son John Rose Holden spent many years in New South Wales, Australia but died in Worcester and was buried at Whittington on May 5th 1860 aged 50, the south chancel memorial window is his.

It was Hyla Holden who, at the Easter Vestry meeting in 1870, proposed that a window be set up to the memory of John Walker, chapel warden from 1831 to 1863. Its central position on the north side of the nave suggests that this is where John Walker sat.

On July 31st 1874 Hyla Holden, Under-Sheriff of Worcester, died aged 58. He too was buried at Whittington, and his memorial window in the nave probably marked his favoured pew on the south side.

REAR ADMIRAL HERBERT BRACE POWELL (1785-1857)

There are many reminders of Rear Admiral Brace Powell in Whittington Church. The most impressive is the monument, by Stephens, on the north wall. His will was dated May 5th 1856 and there is much to thank him for with his legacies to the church.

Herbert Brace Powell was born in Newtown, Herefordshire, but after service as a Captain in the French Wars he returned to live in Worcester. He called his home in London Road Heron Lodge after H.M.S. Heron, the vessel which was commanded by him in the French Wars. In 1816 he commanded H.M.S. Impregnable in the Battle of Algiers. He was present at the dedication of the new Whittington Church in 1844 as Captain Powell, R.N. Later in the 1840's he was promoted to Rear Admiral and with a Grant of Arms took his motto "Impregnable".

He died on December 20th 1857, a letter to John Walker, the Churchwarden at the time, details his two legacies to the church. The first is a legacy of £200 directing the *"interest to be applied forever towards the repair of Whittington Chapel and repair of the monument erected to my memory, provided my body is not disturbed or removed from the said chapel"*. This proviso was to be of great interest, in May 1997 when the church was re-ordered. As the altar was being moved forward, Brace Powell's outer vault was uncovered in the sanctuary. Photographs of it were taken for posterity before it was reinstated.

The second legacy of £80 was for the purchase of a clock for the use of Whittington Chapel. This clock is assiduously wound twice a week, and much time is spent regulating it. It is not known why it points in a westerly direction from its position high in the tower. A permanent marble tablet, also by Stephens, giving notice of his gifts is to be found on the West wall of the church.

JOHN WALKER (1794-1863)

John Walker was Chapel Warden from 1831 to 1863 and the commemorative stained glass window on the north side of the nave and the plaque in the Church are a reminder of his time as church warden, and the generosity he showed in the rebuilding of the Chapel.

On July 25th 1842 following the laying of the corner stone of the new Chapel by Rev. William Rose Holden, John Walker and his wife Elizabeth entertained 200 guests to lunch in a marquee on the lawn at Walkers Place. There were speeches, toasts and dancing. That evening in the marquee the Walkers feasted the local labourers and cottagers, while the workmen engaged on the Church were feasted in the Swan Inn at John Walker's expense, as is quoted in the Berrows Journal of July 28th 1842: -

> *"Thus the clergy and laity, high and low, rich and poor, were abundantly supplied by the bounty of a private gentleman whose excellent and christian example we could wish to see more generally imitated".*

A large room had already been fitted up at the back of Walkers Place where a service had been held the previous day. That room continued to be Whittington's temporary Church until the consecration of the new building on March 19th 1844.

ABRAHAM EDWARD PERKINS (1808-1873)

Abraham Edward Perkins, the Church architect, was buried in the churchyard in April 1873, aged 65, but little is known about his early life. He was a pupil of Rickman of Birmingham but is virtually unknown outside Worcestershire. Whittington was his first commission, which he planned, in the Early English Style, receiving a 5% architect's commission, which amounted to £39.14s.0d. It must have been a proud moment when he and the builder, Mr. Drake of Henwick, led the procession to the site of the Church to see the corner stone being laid. It took twenty months for the new stone Chapel, as we know it, to be rebuilt on the same ground plan and with a similar roof structure. Few of the graves in the churchyard were disturbed, but it seems that only the monuments, engraved slab-stones and the font were returned to the new Chapel.

Perkins was then appointed to be the Cathedral architect in 1845, but in 1859 Sir Gilbert Scott was brought in to complete the restoration with him. Although Perkins was the architect for other churches such as Little Witley in 1868, it was to Whittington that he brought his fourteen-year-old daughter, Anne Maria Perkins, in 1863 to be buried. At that time he was probably living in Sidbury. He died at his home in College Yard in April 1873 and was buried at Whittington by Canon Ryle Wood on April 19th. There are very few other details to be found about him, but Whittington was always his favourite church.

MRS HENRY WOOD

On March 17th 1836, Ellen Price of St. Peter's Worcester was married to Henry Wood of St. Vedast, Foster Lane, London at Whittington. He was a banking and shipping magnate and she was to become famous as Mrs. Henry Wood the Victorian novelist, drawing on the memories of her early years in Worcester for many of her stories.

Her paternal grandparents are buried at Whittington, William Price "of Sidbury" on April 27th 1821, and Mary Price "of London Road" on February 20th 1829. Their son Thomas Price was Ellen's father, and her mother Elizabeth came from Grimley. She was the eldest of eleven children, five boys and six girls. Three of the girls died before the age of two and are buried at Whittington, which was then a chapel in St. Peter's parish and chosen by the Price family for baptisms, marriages and burials.

Her five brothers all attended the King's School between 1826 and 1838 with the School and its environs featuring in the books she began writing after her marriage. After living in France for 20 years, they returned to England, settling in Norwood, London.

Ellen's first novel 'Danesbury House' won her a £100 prize from the Scottish Temperance Society and took its title from the actual name of the family's Sidbury home, which was demolished in 1889. The present three storied building houses Bygones antique shop and carries a plaque, which commemorates the site's connection with Mrs Henry Wood.

The most famous of her novels are The Channings, in which Worcester is Helstoneleigh, Mildred Arkell in which Worcester is Westerbury and East Lynne. In all she wrote about 40 novels selling quite literally millions of copies.

Mrs. Henry Wood died on February 10th 1887 at the age of 73 and was buried at Highgate Cemetery where a red granite monument marks her grave. She is also commemorated in the north transept of Worcester Cathedral where a tablet to her memory depicts her portrait in slight relief on a marble panel.

The Marble tablet and inscription in Worcester Cathedral reproduced by kind permission of the Dean and Chapter of Worcester (LW)

IN MEMORY OF
Mrs HENRY WOOD
A NATIVE OF WORCESTER B. 1814 – D. 1887
AUTHORESS OF MANY WORKS OF FICTION
WHICH HAVE MADE THIS CITY AND CATHEDRAL
KNOWN THROUGHOUT THE ENGLISH-SPEAKING WORLD.
THIS MONUMENT WAS ERECTED IN COMMEMORATION OF THE CENTENARY OF HER BIRTH.

THE CHAPELRY

These two views are taken from sale particulars for this 'delightful small Jacobean country residence' prepared by local auctioneers Bentley, Hobbs and Mytton (RP)

The auction sale took place at The Crown Hotel, Worcester on Monday May 2nd 1949 (RP)

The property remains largely unaltered as can be seen from this 1980's view (RP)

CHURCH LANE

High Walls and Church
Terrace as they appeared
c1909 (P&S/EB)

Rear view of the 'Back-to-Back' Church Terrace c1909 (P&S/EB)

Mrs. Holloway pictured outside her house
3 Church Terrace c1920 (EB)

'High Walls' photographed early in 1930's (PG)

Mick Tanner astride a Royal Enfield motorcycle pictured with his father Jack outside the Church, opposite their home at Church Farm in the late 1940's (BH)

WALKERS LANE

This road was once called Dog Rose Lane. It took its modern name from John Walker (1794 - 1863) and from Walker's Place, the red brick house which he built in the 1820's and lived in for the rest of his life. By 1838 he was farming 104 acres north of the lane and 29 acres at Chapel Farm south of it. In 1865-6 his widow sold Walker's Place to George Chamberlain, a maltster, and he or his son Robert re-named it The Elms.

George Chamberlain had been a churchwarden in St. Peter's and as the new owner of Walker's Place, he had laid claims to John Walker's church pew. He was furious when this was not granted and after much argument he referred his claim to the Bishop in 1868. The Bishop gave judgement against him. One cannot be sure, but this may have been why the house was re-named.

The Grange, Walkers Lane, Whittington 1909 (P&S/EB)

Walkers Lane 1960's close to the point at which Swinesherd Way now divides the lane (LW)

43

ROYAL CELEBRATIONS

QUEEN VICTORIA'S GOLDEN JUBILEE 1887

It was on June 20th 1837 that William IV died and an 18-year-old Queen Victoria ascended the throne. After the death of her husband Prince Albert in 1861, she had largely retired from public view, however, the fiftieth anniversary of her accession was seen as an opportunity to draw her out, as well as a natural occasion for rejoicing. Towns and villages all took up the theme, and Whittington was no exception. Parish Meetings were held in the Schoolroom on May 10th and 16th 1887 to establish a Committee to collect subscriptions. That Committee collected the sum of £35.2s.11d. The day's festivities are recorded in Mr. S.B. Garrard's minutes in the Whittington Chapel Minute Book, now in the Record Office:

> *"The Celebration was held on Thursday 16th June and commenced with a service in the Church, the band from Norton Barracks leading the procession there and back. Afterwards everyone adjourned to the Schoolyard, a row of rick sheets were erected and tables laid for 300. Cold dinner was provided with hot plum pudding, beer and cider, and afterwards a tea for the children and women. The Band from the Barracks played during the day. The provisions consumed were as follows: - 340lbs of meat at 8d., 120 plum puddings, 35 loaves, 20 dozen Ginger Beer, 36 gallons beer, a hogshead of Cider. A sports Committee was formed under the guidance of Mr. S.B. Garrard and a very good programme was gone through, the sports being held on a field adjoining the school, £2.10s.6d. being distributed in prizes. £1 was also spent in presents for the children and each child received a Jubilee Medal and £2 was spent for a Punch and Judy show. On 21 June coloured lights and fireworks were let off on Crookbarrow Hill in response to those from the Worcestershire Beacon".*

QUEEN VICTORIA'S DIAMOND JUBILEE 1897

Ten years later the Queen was still reigning at the grand age of 78. With the experience of 1887 behind them, the villagers knew what to do. A Parish Meeting in the school on May 6th decided on "a Dinner to all residents in the parish over 18 years of age and a Tea to all those under that age". The collection this time totalled £33.8s.4d. and a grant of £2.13s.4d. was made by the Worcester Corporation for the Children. The same Mr. S.B. Garrard again recorded the event in the Whittington Chapel Minute Book.

> *"The Celebration took place on the 24th day of June. The proceedings commenced with a short service in the Church and at 2pm a Dinner consisting of Roast and Boiled Beef, Roast Mutton, Ham, Potatoes and Plum Pudding, Beer and Cider, were served under some rick sheets erected in the yard of the school. About 150 persons sat down to dinner. At 4.30pm about 170 women and children sat down to tea. During the afternoon and evening the Peopleton Band played and Athletic Sports took place and prizes to the value of £3 were distributed. A grant of £2.13s.4d. was obtained from the Corporation of Worcester for the Benefit of the School Children out of which a memorial mug was purchased and presented to each child attending the Village School and the remainder was applied towards defraying the cost of the tea. The provisions consumed were as follows: - 208lbs of Beef and Mutton, 80lbs Bread, 100lbs pudding, 54 gallons Beer, 32 gallons Cider, 50oz Tobacco. This was exclusive of what was consumed at the tea, which was provided by Mr. Cousens of Worcester at 6d. per head".*

KING GEORGE V SILVER JUBILEE

King George V succeeded his father King Edward VII in March 1910, and his Silver Jubilee was celebrated in March 1935.

Herbert March, as Chairman of the Parish Council and Chapel Warden, called a Parish Meeting in the school to decide what to do. There was a service in Church followed by sports in Whittington Meadow and a great sit-down tea. The 155 who had tea were charged 2s. each. The rest cost £30.17s.11d. of which all but the Parish Council's grant of £12 had come from subscriptions.

QUEEN ELIZABETH II CORONATION

Whittington was typical of a small community where almost everyone helps. The 342 inhabitants raised more than £200 in cash and kind to provide for the Village Coronation festivities in the school field on June 2nd 1953. What is more, Whittington had the only ox roast in the Worcester area.

A telegram expressing loyal greetings was sent to the Queen early in the day. Mr. Stuart Limrick began roasting the ox, which had been given by local farmers, over an open wood fire at around 9am. The main programme opened in the afternoon with a service conducted by the Curate, Rev. J.O.C. Champion and the Rector, Rev. A.P. Taylor, gave the address. The cool wind and occasional drizzle did nothing to dampen the festivities, some of which took place in the large marquee.

There were children's and adults' sports followed by a tea in the school for about 100 children. Around 40 old age pensioners also enjoyed tea laid on for them in the school. Mrs. Hoyle, wife of Mr. J.L. Hoyle the Chairman of the organising committee, then presented souvenirs to the children. These consisted of a 5s. Coronation piece and a mug or a book. Susan Edwards presented Mrs. Hoyle with a bouquet of roses and sweet peas. The field activities continued with a tug of war, comic cricket and football matches and an ankle competition.

Mr. Hoyle carved the first slice of beef and presented it to Mr. Dan Mills who, at 81, was the oldest inhabitant present. A bar was provided, which allowed the revellers to toast the Queen, while a Ministry of Food mobile canteen, which was manned by three members of the W.V.S., served tea and sandwiches. The evening's festivities continued with a variety show in the marquee by members of the Young People's Club. This was followed by dancing in the school and the evening concluded with a firework display.

Under the Chairmanship of Mr. Hoyle, the organising committee comprised Rev. J.O.C. Champion, Mr. R.A. Constance (Treasurer), Mr. W.J. Wood (Hon Secretary), Mr. J.C. Baker, Mr. E. Johns, Mr. A.E. Wilkes, Mr. K.H. Lock, Mrs. W. Spreckley, Mrs. R. Dean, Mrs. Lock and Miss Cole. We are fortunate to have a photographic record of Whittington's Coronation Celebrations and a programme detailing the day's activities.

CORONATION
YEAR
1953

Whittington Coronation Celebrations

June 2nd

The Parishioners of Whittington extend their loyal salutations and heartfelt wishes for a long and glorious reign to Her Gracious Majesty Queen Elizabeth II

Programme

4—4.30 p.m.	OPEN AIR SERVICE Conducted by THE REV. CHAMPION
4.30—5 p.m.	CHILDREN'S SPORTS
5—6 p.m.	(a) ADULTS' SPORTS (b) CHILDREN'S TEA (c) PENSIONERS' TEA
6 p.m.	PRESENTATION OF SOUVENIRS to the Children of the Parish
6.15—6.30 p.m.	TUG-OF-WAR . . Men v. Women
6.30 p.m.	BAR OPENS AND CARVING OF OX COMMENCES
7—7.30 p.m.	COMIC CRICKET MATCH
7.30—8 p.m.	ANKLE COMPETITION GREASY POLE WHEELBARROW RACE
8—8.30 p.m.	COMIC FOOTBALL MATCH
8.30—10.30 p.m.	VARIETY SHOW IN THE MARQUEE
9 p.m. onwards	DANCING IN THE VILLAGE SCHOOL
10.30 p.m.	FIREWORK DISPLAY

Rev. J.O.C. Champion (curate) and Rev. A.P. Taylor conduct the open air service.

General view of festivities in Whittington Meadow

The W.V.S. Mobile Canteen doing a brisk trade.

Jack Hoyle, Chairman of the organising committee

Left and Centre:- Reg Constance and J.C. Baker. Members of the organising committee

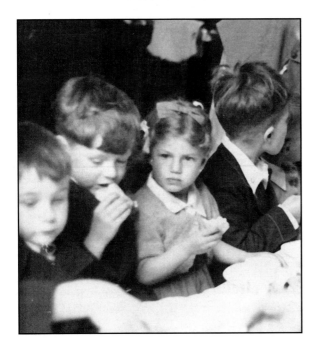

Children's tea in the schoolroom

Mrs. Hoyle presenting souvenirs to the children

Mr. Stuart Limrick tending the ox roast

Eager Villagers awaiting the carving of the Coronation ox.

A happy band of onlookers

Mr. Stuart Limrick and son Tony

Tony Limrick turning the spit

Mr. J. Hoyle and Stuart Limrick carve the first slice

Dick Edwards and Rex Dean man the Bar

The 'greasy pole' competition

Pulling the first pint

Potato peeling
competition

Villagers enjoying
the festivities

The children's sports

The comic cricket match

The crowd enjoying the match

(All Coronation photographs courtesy of AEW/I)

Last ball of the match

QUEEN ELIZABETH II SILVER JUBILEE

The Silver Jubilee of Queen Elizabeth II was celebrated nationally on Tuesday June 7th 1977. A Silver Jubilee Committee chaired by Albert Morris made the plans for Whittington's celebrations.

Having first collected £500 to cover all expenses they staged a mammoth bonfire on Whittington Tump at 10pm on Monday June 6th. A hundred or so people, bearing torches, filed up the Tump, lighting the beacon when Bredon Hill and the Malverns started theirs. The next day the Crookbarrowers laid on a lavish hot luncheon in a suitably decorated Village Hall for all the pensioners. The Church then filled for a 2.00pm service taken by Rev. Cedric Robinson. A recorded peal of bells rang out from the church tower courtesy of some speakers installed there by John Wilkes.

This service was followed by sports organised by the Cricket Club as part of a Fete with many side-shows. In the evening a dance took place in the road outside The Swan, under awnings (not rick sheets!)

In addition the Committee had in April asked Mr. Michael Craze to research and write a History of the Village. This he did, it was printed in December and a free copy delivered to every house in the parish before Christmas.

THE VILLAGE SCHOOL

The first Church of England School at Whittington was built by subscription in 1859. It was built on a site purchased from Thomas Hooke for the sum of £75, and was located off the main road but reasonably close to the church.

The school photographed in 1955 (JA)

Prior to 1859, the only lessons generally available outside the home were taught in the Church Sunday School, which was held in the Church on Sunday mornings and afternoons. For that reason the Village School was commonly referred to as the Day School. School attendance was dependent on the parents, but compulsory once they had registered the child, a fee of two pennies per week was charged.

The Vicar of St. Peter's, Rev. W. Wright, recognised the need for a school in this rural part of his parish, the site of the school being conveyed by deed dated November 26th 1859. According to the records of The National Society, a letter from Rev. W. Wright dated August 1860 states "I have now succeeded with difficulty in building a school for the rural part of my parish".

The earliest school log book dates from February 5th 1869. At this time the school consisted of one room 37 feet long by 17 feet wide, with a gallery and was in the charge of Miss Matilda Cooke, a certified mistress, who was assisted by a monitor whom she instructed at the end of the school day. Miss Fanny Clifton took a great interest in the school and appointed a lady from the village to teach needlework. Miss Clifton's frequent visits to the school were no doubt looked forward to by the scholars to whom she gave a variety of gifts including material, wool, books, baskets of fruit and a workbox for the girl who did the best work. To mark the end of the school year in 1869, Miss Clifton gave the children 'a treat'.

The Rev. E. Robinson, curate of St. Peter's, visited on Mondays, Wednesdays and Fridays to teach religious knowledge and sometimes to take a class in reading. The teachers main task appears to have been preparing the children for the annual examination every February, the outcome of which determined the annual grant. Miss Cooke would have been pleased with the 1870 report which stated: -

> "A marked improvement is noted in the state of this school since my last visit. The teaching is much more vigorous and animated and the answers are given with more promptitude and intelligence".

The 1871 report was even more complimentary;

> "The condition of the school is remarkably good and reflects much credit on Miss Cooke"

and went on to agree the appointment of Miss Fanny Ewins as a pupil teacher.

Miss Cooke resigned in December 1872 and was succeeded by Louisa Rowley in January 1873. The Inspector's report for 1873, however, recommended that more attention be given to the infants and the first standard and concluded by stating: -

> "My Lords will expect a much more favourable report on the instruction of the younger children as a condition of an increased grant".

There seemed to be more occasional holidays during 1873 than in previous years. The children had, as before, one week at Christmas and Easter, four weeks "hay making" holiday in August and half days for Ash Wednesday and Ascension Day. Extra days were allowed in this year for Pershore Fair, Worcester Races, Worcester Toy Fair, Potato Hoeing and Crow Scaring! Also school closed for several days due to heavy falls of snow.

In 1880 June (or Jane) Maund commenced her duties as Mistress and Rev. B.H. Dixon had replaced Rev. Robinson. The Rev. Wright continued to visit regularly to test progress in religious knowledge. The 1880 logbook gives an indication of the number of pupils at school in an entry stating: -

> "only 67 present today due to an outbreak of measles".

Attendance was particularly irregular at this time because of the inability of parents to pay the 'school pence' due to unemployment in the district.

June (or Jane) Maund left the school to get married at the end of the summer term in 1880 and was replaced by Charlotte Chaplin on September 4th 1881. Miss Chaplin took over the school in 'low condition' following several changes of mistress, pupil teachers and monitors in the year before her appointment.

The 1883 report was very flattering and deserves being quoted.

> "This school is excellently managed and taught. The Mistress has great aptitude and skill for Instructing, and no less diligence and perseverance. Consequently the pupils are some of the brightest village children I have ever seen, and do their work with a keenness and accuracy united with unusual intelligence that is most satisfactory. The only weak point at all is a little of the arithmetic in the fourth standard. All the rest is excellent. The sewing is good. The infants are very bright and orderly, and quite as well taught as the older scholars. Indeed I could hardly ask them questions on objects and common things quick enough so sharp and very sure they were with their answers. The excellent 'Merit Grade' may be recommended.

Presented for examination	*40*
Passes in Reading	*40*
Passes in Writing	*40*
Passes in Arithmetic	*32*

H.M Inspector"

Interior of the school as it was in 1955 (WRO)

Miss Clifton's visits to the school had now become very irregular and ceased altogether in 1885. On January 25th 1888 the entry in the logbook reads: -

> *"Closed the school this afternoon in order that myself and the children might attend the funeral of Miss Clifton, the Chief Benefactress of the school and village. We collected and bought a nice cross of flowers to place on her grave".*

In December 1888 Miss Chaplin resigned and was succeeded by Miss Milward who maintained the high standards for the next three years. Miss Annie Williams took up her duties as Mistress in January 1892.

The number of children on the roll rose to 128 by 1894, far too many for the cramped conditions provided by the single classroom and gallery. The Rev. W. Wright had already applied to The National Society for a grant towards the costs of an extension, and a new classroom measuring 21ft by 18ft was added. An assistant teacher was appointed to take responsibility for the new class. Under the 1902 Act Whittington became a voluntary school and was rate aided. The Local Education Authority being responsible for secular instruction while the vicar controlled the religious teaching. The maintenance of the building, provision of books and equipment and staff salaries became charges on the local authority.

The War of 1914-1918 had little effect on the daily routine. Entries in the log show teachers and pupils contributed to national needs. So great was the number of war savings purchased in 1917 that a day's holiday was awarded. Seven hundred weight of horse chestnuts were collected, parcels of magazines, fruit and eggs were sent to military hospitals. The whole school closed for half a day in order that the children could take part in "The Blackberry Scheme" with the total weight collected reaching 10cwt 2qtrs 2lbs!

On April 1st 1930 Whittington was re-organised as a Junior School with scholars over the age of 11 being transferred to city schools, boys going to St. Peter's and girls to Red Hill.

In September 1939 war came again to Britain and the school closed for one week. When the school re-opened on September 11th 1939, nineteen evacuee children from Somerville Junior Mixed School in Birmingham were accepted, a fortnight later seven more joined them. The only interruption caused by the war was the closure of the school for a week in early 1940 due to a shortage of coke for heating, and was only re-opened when a loan was made by the church. Again the children made their contributions to the national effort by knitting socks, gloves and scarves for soldiers, collecting books and purchasing saving certificates.

Following the 1944 Act more free places became available in Secondary Grammar Schools while those selected for the Secondary Modern School were transferred to Pershore.

On December 6th 1950, Whittington Church of England School became a controlled school, with religious education being provided from an agreed syllabus and not limited to the beginning of the day.

The 1944 Act also increased the provision of school milk, which was first introduced in 1934 under the Milk Marketing Board's "Milk Club", and school meals. The first school meals were served at Whittington on February 28th 1951.

As with many other village schools, Whittington did not measure up to the new look in education. The big room on the north side had no windows at eye level and a detached block of earth closets provided the only toilet facilities.

Whittington School Group c1900 (RJ)

Whittington School Group 1928 (RJ)

Scholars of Whittington School 1931 (PM)

63

Another school group from the 1930's. Church Terrace is in the right background and the row of cottages, now demolished, which stood in School Walk, are clearly visible (SSC/LH)

Whittington School Group 1949 - 50 (PG)

A Souvenir Portrait

SCHOLASTIC SOUVENIR CO. LTD., BLACKPOOL.

WHITTINGTON Jun. C.E. SCH.
WORCESTERSHIRE.

1910 - 1935

Silver Jubilee Year of their Majesties, the King & Queen.

(SSC/JT)

A group of pupils pictured in the early 1950's (PG)

A 1950's production of 'HIAWATHA' at Whittington School (PM)

66

The school was rebuilt during 1955, the children being taken by bus to Stoulton School, and was re-opened in January 1956. On July 23rd 1957 a service of re-dedication was held, with Rev. Walters performing the ceremony. The headmistress during this time was Miss Daisy Cole (1949-1960), but she only had some forty pupils on roll, the numbers having dwindled since the peak in the 1890's.

The new school building in 1956 (JA)

In January 1961 Mr. John Appleton took up the position of head teacher, under him numbers increased due in part to the new houses built on the 'Kilbury Drive' estate providing more pupils. It is interesting to note that Mr. Appleton was the first male headteacher in the school's history. In 1975 a crisis arose in that Whittington School had always been in the Pershore District which was now going over to a three-tier system. The new Drakes Broughton Middle School would have taken all children over nine years of age and then passed them on to Pershore High School at fourteen. The seven governors, with Rev. Cedric Robinson as Chairman, avoided this by transferring to the Southern Division of the City where no three-tier system threatened.

The L.E.A. had already said that they could not afford a necessary extension to the infant's classroom, so, in 1978, a band of parent volunteers led by Mr. David James and Mr. Appleton did the work themselves in their own time. The County purchased a part of the adjacent Whittington Meadow to provide a small, but much needed, playing field. Seventy-one pupils were on roll at this time.

Mr. Appleton's own interests were reflected in the school's sporting activities with football and cricket being played and good use made of the swimming pool at The College for the Blind. The school won an award sponsored by Coca-Cola as every pupil in the school could swim. He retired on July 23rd 1982 after twenty-one years as head teacher. A tea party was held outside with staff, pupils, past and present, parents and friends.

Mrs. Millie Ranford was made Acting Head Teacher for the Autumn Term 1982.

On January 4th 1983, Mr. David Holt commenced as Head Teacher at Whittington, with sixty-four pupils on roll.

With Information Technology taking an increasingly important role in today's curriculum it is interesting to note that in September 1984 Whittington Primary School installed its first computer, a BBC Acorn, paid for by the friends of the school. Today in 2000 the children have access to a total of 10 computers and are linked to the Internet, how times have changed!

In 1986 the kitchen used for serving hot meals to the children, was converted to a staff room, the boiler house was also re-equipped and a new heating system installed. During 1987 talks were held on the 'likely' expansion of the school, however the proposed extension was to be a larger mobile classroom and a further building to provide another classroom. This would raise the possible admission number to 107. In July of 1989 a double mobile classroom arrived, the school had 90 children on roll and four members of staff.

Near the end of the Autumn Term in 1994, the usual Christmas services and parties were held. School Christmas lunch was enjoyed at the Village Hall with a wonderful cooked meal for everyone of turkey and vegetables followed by dessert, all prepared by Mrs. Brown, Mrs. Robertson, Mrs. Bampfield, Mrs. Wiltshire and a team of very cheerful helpers. This was to be the last Christmas party in the village hall as by the following year they had moved into the new school buildings and the numbers on roll were too high to continue this small village school custom. With the new extension complete, the building was officially handed over to the Head Teacher. Classes 1-4 moved into a new building and class 5 along with the secretary, Mrs. Wynn, moved across to the mobile classrooms whilst the renovations to the old part of the school were carried out and both parts linked with the new foyer. This meant that the entrance to the school was now reached from a new access road constructed opposite the Swan Inn in Old Road.

In March 1995 the second phase of the school building was handed over. On March 11th there was an official opening by the Bishop of Worcester, Right Rev. Philip Goodrich. This gave the school four extra classrooms and for the first time in it's history a hall which also doubled up as a gymnasium. By the summer term of 1995, there were 117 pupils on roll. In the spring term of 1996, a three-day Ofsted inspection took place, which reported the school to be performing very well. In February 1997 Mr. Holt appointed Mr. Ken Smith to produce a wood carving for the new building. During this month Mr. Smith became the artist in residence for a week and worked with the children. The final piece being erected on the wall outside the hall for all to enjoy.

Having settled into the new school building the school staff and PTA began planning to develop the school grounds. A garden project was planned to provide an outdoor classroom area for the infants, covered seating areas and planting of more trees to provide areas of shade for the children during the summer months. A school pond was also excavated.

In the Autumn Term of 1998, a second Ofsted team came to inspect the school and again it received a very favourable report. A typical comment from the report being that the children were found to be happy and well disciplined at this school. The numbers of pupils on roll by this time was 184 and with new staffing appointments bringing the total of staff to 12 an extension to the staff room was required.

1999 saw the number of pupils maintained and further progress made with the landscaping of the school grounds. The school celebrated the New Millennium with each child planting a daffodil bulb in the school grounds; a school tea towel was also produced which featured the face of every pupil. Furthermore a special commemorative book was compiled in which each pupil wrote his or her hopes and wishes for the New Millennium.

Spring Term 2000 saw 197 pupils on the roll, with 8 teaching and 14 supporting staff busily employed at the school.

Whittington Church of England Primary School. School Group - 1999 (BPC)

WHITTINGTON HALL - MIDLANDS ELECTRICITY TRAINING COLLEGE

On a seven-acre site purchased in 1901, Mr. John Ratcliffe built himself Whittington Hall, an Edwardian mansion of yellow Stourport brick. Above its reception rooms and kitchens seven bedrooms were provided, with servants quarters on the floor above that. The bathrooms boasted hot and cold running water and the building was wired for electricity. Outside there were stables, a coach house, two paddocks and a tennis lawn. The short drive being adorned by the yellow brick entrance lodge and walled garden. The Ratcliffes lived there until 1911 and then let it to Colonel H.S. Barlow for ten years. It was then sold to Mr. Edward Fownes Rigden, a director of Fownes Gloves Ltd, who added the next field to the estate, which it is still known as Rigden's.

On the outbreak of war in September 1939 the property was requisitioned by the War Office for the training of women soldiers of the Auxiliary Territorial Service (A.T.S.) who were boarded there. Later it became the ante-natal refuge and clinic of unmarried ATS mothers. When in 1944 the War Office no longer needed it, the whole estate was bought by the National Institute for the Blind who intended to bring their young blind boys from Chorleywood in Hertfordshire and set up a single 8 to 19 years old boarding school. However, after the 1945 General Election the Labour Minister of Education forbade any secondary school to be linked to a primary school so killing the N.I.B. plan. Already Mr. Herbert Clarke, Senior Master at the College for the Blind, was living in the Lodge and the Ministry of Agriculture rented the rest, having displaced persons there for land work. Finally in May 1950 the N.I.B. sold Whittington Hall to the Midlands Electricity Board, the Lodge too was sold some 12 years later.

The newly-formed M.E.B. made Whittington Hall the headquarters of their Worcestershire Sub Area. When in 1959 a move to offices in Worcester's Blackpole Road became necessary it provided the company with the opportunity to use the Hall as a residential training centre. Mr. J.G. Wood was Warden, and Miss Jean Archer was matron. In 1971-72 the number of bedrooms increased by the addition of a new block, this time in pale red brick, a training shop was also added. Mr. Geoff Wood took early retirement in 1976, emigrating to America where he married an American woman he had met on a previous holiday in the States. Miss Jean Archer retired in 1977 after 18 years at the college; she too left the area, moving to a new home in York.

In 1986 planning permission was granted for the transfer of Overhead Training to Whittington from its site in Shropshire. The necessary poles went up in the adjacent fields, a new canteen was built and the kitchen refurbished. In 1987 Mr. Tony Wallis arrived as site manager, since then the number of bedrooms has been increased and lecture rooms and a conference hall has been added. Great care has been taken over the landscaping of these developments and the view of it from the A44 is relatively unspoilt.

In January 2000, Pemberstone Plc, a Worcester property management company, took control of the site, part of which is being leased back to Midlands Electricity.

Mr. J.G. Wood outside the front entrance to Whittington Hall in 1959 (MEB)

THE COLLEGE FOR THE BLIND - (RNIB NEW COLLEGE)

It was a King's School mathematics master, Rev. R.H. Blair, who in 1866 started the "Blind College for the Sons of Gentlemen" in the Sidbury wing of the Commandery. He did so because between June 1862 and June 1865 Norman McNeile, a boy blind from birth, had been a boarder at Blair's King's School house and he had seen what the new Braille system for reading and writing could do for the blind. McNeile went on to Trinity College, Dublin in 1866, gained a first in Theology in 1870 and became a parish priest in Yorkshire, where his father was Dean of Ripon. In 1887 the College moved from the Commandery and rented Slaughters Court at Powick, a property belonging to Earl Beauchamp. The Rev. Samuel S. Forster M.A. was headmaster from 1872 until his death in April 1891. The move to Whittington came in 1902 through the benevolence of Mrs. Eliza Warrington who bought the land from the Sebrights in 1896 and later gave the College £8,000 to build a boarding school there.

The College for the Blind - c1916 (P&S/EB)

"The College for the Blind" became internationally famous under the headmastership of George Clifford Brown (1913-1938). He was a very good chess player and made it the college's main game, one of the boys, R.W. Bonham, became English Amateur Champion and returned to teach at the college (1929-1969). Brown had the boys rowing on the Severn and even racing at Henley, they had their own Scout Troop and every boy learned to swim in the College pool, opened in 1925. Also in 1925 an athletics track was constructed on land opposite the college, alongside the A44 Whittington Road. This facility, which was also used by the village school, served the college well until the widening of the A44 into a dual carriageway made it less accessible despite the provision of the footbridge.

The sports ground, with its cinder track and football pitch, was situated between Walkers Lane and the government buildings. The site was eventually used to accommodate the residential developments of Whitewood Way and Whitewood Close. On August 14th 1936 the National Institute for the Blind took responsibility for the College's finances, until then dependant on fees and gifts. The institution then spent £25,000 on a new wing which Earl Baldwin of Bewdley, the former Prime Minister, opened in 1939 as the Baldwin Wing. That year was Brian Oswald Bradnack's first year as headmaster (1939-59) who, like Brown, lived at The Gables, which had been bought in 1922. He now had the Second World War to contend with, no easy matter with fifty blind boys. However, one consolation came with the 1944 Education Act, which empowered Local Authorities in England and Wales to send blind boys of grammar school ability to the Worcester College for the Blind and girls to the National Institute's sister school at Chorleywood, Hertfordshire, and pay their fees. As a result some very clever boys came to the College from far afield and Mr. Bradnack was able to insist on a high entry standard.

Richard Cawthorne Fletcher (1959-80) succeeded Bradnack in 1959 and it was under him on June 7th 1962 that Princess Margaret arrived by helicopter to open the Wolfson Wing. In 1957 the Wolfson Foundation had made a grant of £50,000 and with it a Braille library, science laboratory, craft room, common room and upstairs dormitories were added, together with a compact and beautiful Chapel to seat 100 for which friends and former pupils had subscribed. As Chairman of the Worcester City Magistrates and Headmaster for 21 years, he was awarded the O.B.E. in 1980.

His successor, the Rev. B.R. Manthorp, then had to deal with one of the biggest upheavals in the College's history. The now Royal National Institute for the Blind and the Governors decided to amalgamate the Chorleywood girls with the Worcester boys. The sale of Chorleywood yielded sufficient funds to build new houses and a sixth form centre on the Worcester site, this being completed by 1990. Much of this work has gone towards producing an attractive campus which is an important part of the Whittington area and also included an extensive science wing sponsored by BP.

In May 1993 Anneka Rice from the BBC's Challenge Anneka television programme arrived at RNIB New College, her challenge was to build the world's first sensory maze for blind people. The maze was to have been constructed in just 2½ days, starting from a green-field site. However the project was, in Anneka's words, "totally scuppered" by the weather. Construction was delayed as heavy rain turned the site into a mudbath. The project was not completed within the challenge deadline, but six weeks later Anneka Rice and the cameras returned to the completed maze for the official opening ceremony.

Rev. Robert Manthorp left the college in December 1994, being succeeded by Mrs. Helen Williams, who came to the school with an impressive record as Headteacher in several selective schools, most recently as High Mistress of St. Paul's Girls' School. The college greeted the new millennium with the appointment of Mr. Nick Ratcliffe as the new Principal and continues to have a very high national and international reputation, being recognised as one of the country's top performing schools through its membership of the Headmasters and Headmistresses Conference and the bestowing of Beacon status by the government. Throughout this time of considerable development the college has always remembered its links with the Whittington area and although the college hasn't actually been in Whittington since the boundaries were changed by the City of Worcester (Extension) Order 1931, it has maintained a close link with the village school and enjoyed a social and economic relationship with many Whittington inhabitants.

An aerial view of college and grounds (RNIB)

The college athletic ground with the government buildings clearly visible in the background (RNIB)

RNIB NEW COLLEGE - G.C. BROWN'S HOUSE - formerly THE GABLES

The property formerly known as The Gables had been built for a retired Admiral in the mid-Victorian era. The Admiral must have been wealthy, for the house was constructed of the best glazed russet brick; had seven principal bedrooms, well appointed reception rooms, servants quarters, wine cellar, butler's pantry and a conservatory. Outside was a paved courtyard for the horses adjacent to the coach house, above which were the coachman's quarters. The house featured a magnificent redwood single flight open staircase which eventually led to it becoming a listed building. The dormer windows at roof height gave rise to a quantity of gables, which suggested the name.

School House,
College for the higher Education of the Blind, Worcester.

(RNIB)

Outside were substantial grounds with a croquet lawn and tennis court, and extensive orchards set with the best of both hard and soft fruits including Conference pears, Cox's apples, some scarce whitecurrants and prime gooseberries.

The Admiral must have been waited on in a rather splendid style, however during two particularly hard winters in the 1890's he opened up a free soup kitchen from which his staff fed many villagers who were unable to work in the icy conditions and who would otherwise have had to recourse to the Poor Law.

At around the same time that the College came to Whittington, The Gables passed into the hands of a Worcester solicitor who remained there until 1922, when the college governors were able to purchase the house and grounds for use by the headmaster, who had, like his predecessors for the past 20 years occupied nearly half of the college building.

When in 1977 the Fletchers left The Gables to move to their own property at Wick, near Pershore this Victorian property was in need of complete restoration, after decades of hard wear. There were thoughts of demolishing it and building a modern replacement, but as it was by now a listed building this was not an option. Instead it was decided to adapt it for use by the pupils of the college, where space was becoming ever more precious. All the plumbing and wiring were replaced, large sections of the roof renewed, floors, main timbers and joists were removed and made good and windows copied and replaced. Much work also went into meeting the stringent requirements of the fire authority with some £80,000 being spent in all.

The house now bears the name of George Clifford Brown and is home to some 13 pupils.

BENJAMIN WILLIAMS LEADER RA

The residents of Whittington are justifiably proud that one of the most popular Victorian landscape artists, B. W. Leader RA, resided in the village from 1861 until 1889. First, lodging with Mrs. Doe at Bank Cottage, then briefly at 'Hill End' before purchasing Whittington Lodge next to the church.

Benjamin's family name was Williams. Born on March 12th 1831, he was the third child of eleven children, second son, of Sarah and Edward Leader Williams. His father's profession at the time was an ironmonger with his premises at 94 High Street, Worcester, so one can only assume that Benjamin began his life in the family quarters 'above' the shop.

By 1835 Mr. Williams was calling himself an engineer and became the resident engineer for the Severn Navigational Commission. He, also, was one of the leading cultural patrons of the city; an amateur artist himself.

The family moved twice. First across the River Severn to the parish of St. John's, and then returning back over the river in the late 1840's to Diglis House, now the Diglis House Hotel.

Educated at the Grammar School and Silver Street Academy, Benjamin in 1845, following in his brother's footsteps, entered his father's office to learn engineering but, from the first, sketching in the field was far more to his taste than making plans of river locks and weirs. (His brother, also named Edward Leader Williams after their father, was knighted in 1894 for his work as Chief Engineer on the construction of the Manchester Ship Canal). With the blessing of his father Benjamin left the office and studied at the Worcester School of Design and in December 1853 was accepted by the Royal Academy Schools in London, so founding his lifelong profession. He only studied there a short while, but was lucky enough in his first year to have a picture hung and sold in the Academy's Summer Exhibition. An American purchased it for £50: a large and encouraging price for an unknown artist's work. From that year, 1854, Benjamin exhibited every year (except 1858) until 1923; the year of his death. In 1857 Benjamin changed his surname to Leader (his father's second name) to distinguish himself from the numerous other artists named Williams, exhibiting in London, to whom he was not related. As far as it can be ascertained the artist did not add the second initial 'W' (Williams) until the following year, 1858, perhaps suggesting a degree of discomfort for dropping his family name.

In August 1876 Leader married Mary Eastlake of Plymouth; great niece to Sir Charles Locke Eastlake who had been President of the Royal Academy from 1850 until his death in 1856. The first three of their five children were born at Whittington Lodge. Leader's commitment to the village included supporting the Church in giving part of his property to extend the churchyard on the north side. Two of Leader's sisters were married at the Church. Elizabeth Leader Williams married Edward Cox, an engineer, from Bowden in May 1867 and Marie Patty Leader married Richard Smith-Carington of Barbourne Hall, Worcester in April 1879. Smith-Carington, who had inherited his father's horticultural nursery, established a worldwide seed business and became famous for introducing the Worcester Pearmain apple. The couple were Mayor and Mayoress of Worcester in 1889. This was the year B. W. Leader moved from Whittington to Burrows Cross, near Gomshall, Surrey to be nearer to the Royal Academy. Although he had been elected an Associate Royal Academician in 1883 he still had the burning ambition to become a Royal Academician and this he felt couldn't be achieved in living so far away from London. Leader still had to wait another nine years before his election in 1898.

The City of Worcester did not forget their famous 'son' when, in 1914, he received the Freedom of the City. At the celebratory luncheon at the Guildhall one of the guests was Sir Edward Elgar. During his speech of congratulations to Leader he said some of his music had been inspired by the artist's paintings of the Worcestershire landscape. Like John Constable before, who Leader much admired, he painted best what he knew best and this was, for Leader, Worcestershire's rivers, its leafy lanes, commons and fields, and its villages and churches. Although depicted at different times of the year, the scenes are usually bathed in an amber glow of the setting sun or the harsher brightness of early morning after rain.

Those paintings of Whittington show how rural the village was a century and a half ago. They were usually given generalised titles although a number are identifiable. For example, 'The Outskirts of a Farm', dated 1860, depicts sheep lying about, and hens, chicks and turkeys scratching, in a lane bordered on the right by a sandy bank lined with trees and on the left by timber beamed farm buildings; part of Church Farm.

Others include the once tree lined 'Gypsy Lane', signed only, and 'View of Worcester from Crookbarrow Hill', c1889. The viewpoint of 'Worcester from Whittington', 1878, is from the grounds at Whittington Lodge and depicts the still standing oak tree. Summer scenes of Whittington hayfields are well represented. In 'An English Hayfield', exhibited 1879 at the Royal Academy, amidst the dried hay are figures which, according to Leader, were posed by his wife, their first son, Benjamin, and baby daughter Ethel. Leader's favourite painting, exhibited at the Royal Academy in 1882, was given a proverbial biblical quotation "In the evening it shall be light" for its title. The all too familiar rainy winter day has given away to a brilliant sun-set which illuminates a church and its churchyard which is separated from a rain-soaked field by a dry stone wall. Leader later stated the church was the old fourteenth/fifteenth century Whittington church, demolished in 1842, and its churchyard. Although the church is unlike the existing drawings of the old church, the tombstones and the venerable ancient yew tree in the churchyard are recognisable features today. Closer likenesses of the old church are depicted in an early work 'A Country Church'; Whittington, Worcester of 1861 and 'An April Day' exhibited at the Royal Academy in 1887.

These, as well as his other landscapes, are an important part of our cultural and historical heritage. It is hoped that one day Benjamin Williams Leader RA will be remembered alongside our great British painters.

Benjamin Williams Leader 'at home' at Whittington (RW)

An 1880's view of Whittington Lodge at Haymaking time (KW)

76

Whittington Lodge c1935 with gardener Bert Smith tending borders (PG)

Whittington Lodge and Church c1935 (PG)

BERKELEY CLOSE

The road now known as Berkeley Close was first developed in the 1930's, when the four pairs of semi-detached houses were built. The road then was regarded as an extension of Church Lane and this was reflected in its postal address.

These semi-detached houses were built to replace the row of farm-workers cottages, which were situated on the right a little way down what is now Brewers Lane. The cottages occupied a site close to where some agricultural buildings stand today. It is said that the people who moved into these new houses literally carried their furniture and possessions up the back gardens. These houses must have seemed the height of luxury, offering an inside downstairs toilet and bathroom, and in the garden at the rear a shared brick built wash-house complete with a coal fired water boiler and a little chimney.

An undated painting by W. Stinton of the cottages which stood off what is now
Brewer's Lane, note the well on the far right (AJ)

In the 1950's there was again a need for further housing in the village, so another ten houses were added, this time on the south side. A terrace of four houses facing Church Lane with another terrace of four and a pair of semis facing the original 1930 properties were built and occupied in late 1954 and early 1955. The builders were Sears of Evesham, and the landlords were Pershore Rural District Council.

By 1960 yet more housing was required and a further sixteen dwellings were built comprising of two terraces of four houses on the south side and two pairs of semi-detached bungalows and four maisonettes on the north. These properties were occupied during March 1961, and around this time the road was called Berkeley Close.

In the mid 1980's a private developer built a further five houses at the top of the Close, backing onto the motorway and completed the development of this part of the village.

Construction of the council houses 1955 (WRO)

(PM)

(LW)

Berkeley Close mid 1960's note the Elm trees which dominated the sky line until stricken by Dutch Elm disease in the 1970's

Elm tree being felled, early 1970's at junction of Church Lane and Berkeley Close (LW)

WOODSIDE

The property known as Woodside is situated behind Whittington Hall and accessed by a rough drive, which is a public footpath, between Rigden's field and Whittington Hall. Woodside and its grounds are now in the ownership of Pemberstone Plc.

Woodside and its surrounding orchards was, in the 1920's and 1930's, a commercial fruit growing business. The Kelly's directory of 1922 lists the owner as Ernest Vivian Broad and his occupation as fruit grower. By the late 1930's Woodside was occupied by William and Alice Duggan. The nearby outbuilding was probably used as a store or pack-house, but was also used apparently for the making of jam from the fruit grown in the orchards.

Elizabeth Halfyard (William Duggan's sister) pictured outside Woodside (CS)　　　Elizabeth Halfyard and Alice Duggan outside barn (CS)

Interior of the barn in 1999 (LW)

WHITTINGTON AND DISTRICT WOMEN'S INSTITUTE

The first meeting of Whittington and District W.I. was held in the schoolroom at 7pm on February 23rd, 1939, under the guidance of Mrs. Pedley, a Voluntary County Organiser. The first president was Mrs. Mark Bates and the secretary Mrs. Richardson. Among the founder members were Mrs. Doris Williams, Mrs. Ford and Mrs. Corfield. The last two were to remain members for the rest of their lives and Mrs. Corfield won an award for ten years of unbroken attendance at meetings.

The March meeting was also held in the schoolroom but from April till July the venue was Crookbarrow Farm. In September, just after the outbreak of the Second World War, Mrs. Arnold Webb invited the institute to meet at New Place, Whittington Road. In October the meeting was again at Crookbarow Farm, at 3.30pm. Then, from November onwards the meetings were held once more in the schoolroom, the times varying between 4pm and 7pm.

The first Annual Meeting was held in January 1940 when there were 38 members. The subscription was then 2s. per year but rose to 2s.6d. in 1944, then to 3s.6d. and 5s., increasing steadily over the years to the present level of £15.50!

Wartime activities consisted of canning and jam making (for which sugar was purchased in bulk by the Institute), wartime cookery, knitting, collection of rose hips, salvage and blood donation. One of the talks was on 'Household Jobbery'!

An attempt to start Folk Dancing classes failed through lack of support but there was a choir for some years.

Meetings were held every month but in March 1943 it was decided to hold eleven meetings in the year always in the schoolroom but at varying times, either afternoon or evening. In 1951 the Institute was offered the use of the Ebenezer Baylis canteen as a meeting place. Mrs. Russell Baylis was a long-standing member and embroidered a tablecloth for the president's table, which is still in use, as is the cloth embroidered by Mrs. Doris Wilkes for the Treasurer's table.

In 1954 the Annual Meeting was moved to November and in January 1955 the Institute met for the first time in the new Village Hall where it has met at 2.30pm on the third Thursday of every month, except August, ever since, apart from an occasional Garden Meeting held at members' homes. The institute members were very pleased at last to be able to meet in Whittington itself and are very much at home in the hall, which continues to receive much praise and admiration from visiting speakers.

In 1962 there were 54 members and in 1964 the Institute celebrated its Silver Jubilee and held a dinner in the Village Hall. The Golden Jubilee was celebrated with enthusiasm but sadly a much smaller number of members in 1989 and in February 1999 the Diamond Jubilee was celebrated. It is interesting to note that ten past members have lived to be over ninety years of age and one over a hundred!

Whittington and District W.I. 25th Birthday Celebration February 1964 (MB)

November 6th 1997
Whittington & District W.I. planting a Glastonbury Thorn in the churchyard
extension to commemorate the centenary of the W.I. movement (MB)

WHITTINGTON CRICKET CLUB

Whittington Cricket Club was founded in 1949 although cricket had been played between the two World Wars in a field behind Harkaway in Pershore Road. The field, owned by J.C. Baker, was rather narrow with the pitch being rolled out from what remained of the earlier pitch. Teas were provided at The Swan, but the distance proved rather time consuming. The newly formed club, with Walter Spreckley as president, moved for its second season to the Chapelry field behind the church, near to Mr. Spreckley's home at Whittington Lodge.

This field was farmed by Jack Tanner and like most village pitches at that time had no gang mower for the outfield and relied on an early crop of hay and the grazing of cattle or sheep. This could be quite disconcerting when the field was being strip grazed as two thirds was reasonably short with cowpats and the rest was rough grass. Brian Wilkes recalls a match against the Dominics when a five was run off a lost ball, which was still within the confines of the boundary.

Gentlemen - v - Players - August 12th 1950 (JT)

The club still proceeded to The Swan for teas, where a high standard was set, including cream cakes from Claptons Bakery. For away matches one of Marks' Coaches was hired, picking up at The Swan and various points in the village. These matches provided a most enjoyable Sunday afternoon and evening out with visits to the home team's local pub, and occasionally one or two others on the way back. The club also organised an annual seaside outing for the village, which was always fully booked. In 1954 the Village Hall was opened opposite the Chapelry field, and this provided changing facilities and was much more convenient for teas.

The club enjoyed several seasons on the Chapelry field, where the slight slope favoured Jack Hoyle's quick bowling, and where in 1957 a Trinity Press XI were dismissed for just eight runs! However a dispute between the owner of the field and the tenant over a matter totally unrelated to cricket resulted in the club having to find another ground.

A move to Rigden's field, which was owned by The College for the Blind and farmed by Jack Tanner, was arranged, and a pitch laid in December 1958 at a cost of £60. During the 1959 season all matches were either played away or on hired pitches.

Rigden's field, situated between the M.E.B. Training Centre and the Blind College, saw its first match at the start of the 1960 season. Whilst still having to rely on an early crop of hay, the club purchased a large antiquated and somewhat "temperamental" gang mower. This machine was hand propelled, not sit-on, which made cutting the rough outfield a very strenuous operation. A pavilion was purchased for changing in, but teas were still taken at the Village Hall with the high standards being maintained by the Ladies Committee. The ladies were very much involved in fund raising events for the club, running successful dances and whist drives at the Village Hall. The College headmaster R.C. Fletcher kept wicket and batted in a masterly fashion. In 1965 the Club won the Pershore Village Shield knock-out competition, beating Fladbury in the final.

In 1973 the club had another enforced move when the College for the Blind, wanting to protect their boundaries, swapped the sloping field at the back of the college for Rigden's. The club was fortunate to secure the use of the historic Norton Barracks ground which had only been vacated a year earlier when Worcester City Cricket Club moved to Battenhall.

1974 saw Chris Graham score the club's maiden century at Rushwick and in 1977 Tony George hit two centuries, 104 not out at Cutnall Green and 110 at Bringsty. The second hit the headlines, as he went from 50 to 100 with eight sixes and two singles. For ten years the club maintained the ground, which could be faster than the County Ground, while the surrounding buildings were unoccupied and falling derelict. They had the use of a small pavilion, which had no power or water. Changing facilities and teas were arranged in the skittle alley of the Retreat Public House.

Eventually the Barracks, fields and certain buildings came up for sale, but the club had neither the finance nor the membership to join the consortium, which purchased the complex.

The obvious alternative was the playing field at Norton Parish Hall at Littleworth, which had been opened in 1977. Norton Parish Hall provided the facilities for changing and teas and with help from Norton Parish

A cricket match being played on 'The Paddock', Church Lane (BH)

Council and the Hall Management Committee, coupled with a change of name, the club was again able to enjoy the benefits of village cricket.

Whittington and Norton Cricket Club now had a ground with the outfield mowed, changing and refreshment facilities close at hand and practice nets; pipes were laid for watering the wicket. This was an important feature as the pitch at Norton dried out very quickly and needed a lot of attention to maintain it to a reasonable standard.

The Ladies Committee enjoyed the improved facilities at Norton and continued to provide refreshments on match days and to cater for barbecues, barn dances and other social events. The cricket club organised several successful 'fun-runs' around Whittington, with proceeds going to local charities.

In a move for more competitive cricket a team was successfully entered into the local evening league, but during the early 1990's several key players left the area. There were insufficient younger members keen to play Sunday afternoon friendly matches, which had been the hallmark of the club since its inception. Several attempts were made to recruit new players from the villages without success, but a nomadic side called The Shiremen joined forces in 1993. This swelled the membership but lacked the involvement to work on the wicket. By 1994 standards were dropping while other village sides, who had survived, were improving. It appears that younger players preferred Saturday or mid-week league cricket over the traditional Sunday game.

The keen lads that remained found themselves overworked, as they had to prepare the wicket, organise the playing side etc., and were held back from playing a better standard of cricket themselves. As a result the 1995 season was the last playing season, a sad position after 47 years. The club has remained in existence as a social club with the hope that in the future the younger element in the villages may once again form a playing side.

A 50th year Celebration Dinner held in November 1998 was a reminder of the many successful dinners held since the club's formation, the first at the Diglis Hotel and others at various hostelries including The New Inn at Broughton Hackett, The Star, The Crown and The Talbot. The annual dinner has also been held for many years at Whittington Village Hall with Dawes Caterers providing excellent fare.

The club has been fortunate to have had many loyal and hard working officers over the years. John Tanner was secretary from 1949 to 1965; David Crook then held the post for 21 years, followed by David Watson and Jonathon Harris. Just four secretaries spanning 50 years is mirrored by only four treasurers covering the same period; Reg Constance for 25 years, Michael Braddock for 10, Bruce Mercer for 4 until he left the area and Graham Henderson 11 years to date. The office of Chairman was initially held by Jack Hoyle until 1958 and then by Albert Wilkes until 1978 when he was succeeded by his son Brian Wilkes who holds the office to date.

Captains		Presidents	
1949	Geoff Collins	1949-63	W.F. Spreckley
1950-54	Brian Wilkes	1964-71	J.L. Hoyle
1955	Tony George	1972-73	A.E. Wilkes
1956	Michael Tanner	1974-79	R.A. Constance
1957-60	Brian Wilkes	1980-83	A.B. Morris
1961-68	Michael Braddock	1984-89	W.H. Taylor
1969-70	Chris Graham	1990-91	P.G. Cope
1971-83	Tony George	1992-93	A.N. George
1984-86	Tim Crook	1994-95	M. Braddock
1987-88	Tony George		
1989-90	Spencer Bradley		
1991-92	Paul Bozward		
1993	Ivan Crouchly		
1994-95	Trevor Bedford		

Although not now an active playing club, many long-standing friendships were formed, and still exist due to the Whittington and Norton Cricket Club.

WHITTINGTON AND DISTRICT YOUNG PEOPLE'S CLUB

It was in 1947 that the St. Martin's curate responsible for Whittington, Rev. Keith Wedgewood, together with Horace Gammon decided to form a Youth Club. It had some fifteen members, including Louis Huband and John and Michael Tanner. Their meetings and social functions were held in the village school.

In 1952 under the curate Rev. John Champion, who boarded in the village with Miss Rammell at Bank Cottage, the catchment area was enlarged and the Youth Club became the Whittington and District Young People's Club. Rev. John Champion left Whittington in 1953 to become a Chaplain in the Royal Navy, the Club continued with Joan Johns, Bunty Taylor and John Wilkes as leading members.

Although the headmistress of the school, Miss Daisy Cole, allowed use of the building for meetings and social functions, the venue was far from ideal. All the Club's equipment, tables, chairs etc. were stored in a "lean-to" shed, having to be brought in and returned when the evening's activities were over. Herbert Clarke, Second Master at the Blind College, enabled Club functions to be held at the College in the gymnasium. Dances were held to live bands, but more usually to music provided by their resident "disc jockey" John Wilkes.

With the opening of Whittington Village Hall on November 20th 1954 the Whittington and District Young People's Club had access to the type of facilities they had dreamed of. Bill Evans and a band of helpers constructed a folding stage for the Hall and a drama group, "The Picador Players" was formed. With Horace Gammon as stage manager, The Picador Players became a very accomplished group, even taking their plays 'on tour' to Norton, Inkberrow and other surrounding villages.

Eventually the Whittington and District Young People's Club proved unwieldy; much of its leadership was extra-parochial and it lost impetus. The Whittington members consolidated their efforts forming a new group, the "Crookbarrowers" in 1961. The name, taken from Crookbarrow Hill is said to have been the suggestion of Ken Lock.

A Harvest Supper by Whittington and District Young People's Club held in the old schoolroom in the early 1950's (AEW/BW)

THE VILLAGE HALL

Prior to the building of the present Village Hall local organisations used the village school as a meeting place. This led to problems with equipment having to be taken in and out and tables and chairs moved in each time there was a meeting or social function. As the activities of Whittington and District Young People's Club grew and flourished, there was much more pressure for a more suitable and larger venue. Eventually a committee was set up to explore the possibilities of building a Village Hall.

By the start of the Second World War £435 had been raised and a site next to the school promised by the Berkeleys. Following the interruption of the War years the project was resumed in 1952 and a committee, chaired by Mr. J.C. Baker, then Chairman of the Parish Council, secured the current site from the Berkeleys for £50. Successful fund raising had, by 1954, increased the £435 to £2000, and with this money, an instant utility building seemed better than a purpose built and more expensive one which would have attracted some grant aid.

Construction commenced on an ex-War Department pre-cast concrete framed building with single thickness brick infill panels. Toilet facilities and a very small kitchen were divided off the main hall, and there was a central entrance foyer. The Village Hall was officially opened by the Mayor of Worcester, Mrs Rosa Ratcliffe on November 20th 1954. Heating was by eaves level electric fires which apparently "cooked your head and left your feet cold". The small triangular site afforded very limited car parking.

The Village Hall nearing completion in 1954 (BN/WRO)

Guests arriving for the opening ceremony (AEW/BW)

Whittington residents attending the Village Hall official opening on November 20th 1954 (AEW/BW)

Residents and guests eagerly await the opening of the new Village Hall (AEW/BW)

Mrs. Rosa Ratcliffe, Mayor of Worcester, at the opening of the Village Hall, November 20th 1954 (AEW/BW)

A meeting of Whittington Village Hall Management Committee was held on January 18th 1955.

The elected committee were: -

Chairman	Mr. Hoyle
Treasurer	Mr. Constance
Secretary	Miss Lawrence
Committee	Mrs Wilkes
	Miss Berry
	Mr. Wilson
	Mr. Tanner
	Mr. Lock
	Mr. Gammon

At this meeting, the following scale of charges were agreed for the use of the hall: -

Whittington Young People's Club	
Games evenings, up to 10 o'clock	10/-
Whist drives up to 11 o'clock	25/-
Dances up to 12 o'clock	30/-
Women's Institute meetings	10/-
Cricket Club teas	7/6
Hire by village organisations for committee meetings	
Afternoons	7/6 per hour
Evenings	10/- per hour
Main charges:	
Up to 6 o'clock	10/6 per hour
After 6 o'clock	12/6 per hour
Minimum charge	2 guineas

Time for preparation, before actual hired time, charged at 5/- per hour.

Sunday School tea in the village Hall (Late 1950's) (BN/PM)

The Scene in Whittington Village Hall in September 1958 when Whittington and District Young People's Club
held their annual Harvest Home Supper (IE)

A Village Hall 'do' mid 1960's (JL)

A Summer fete in the 1970's (BH)

The Hall continued in this form until 1974, when a full-length side extension was built providing a new entrance foyer, a committee room and a large well equipped kitchen. The old kitchen walls were demolished and improved toilets provided. In 1978 more land was purchased from the Berkeleys to provide extra car parking and in 1984 the Hall was lengthened providing a secure store room, a stage and storage areas. In 1987 the Village Hall won the Best Kept Village Hall Award for smaller communities sponsored by Calor Gas.

Villagers and committee members celebrate the Best Kept Village Hall Award 1987 (BN/ABM)

A full and varied programme of events is offered with up to three different activities taking place each day.

Whittington Organ Group was formed in 1974 and launched by John Wilkes and Bruce Hodgkins in November of that year, when they decided to hold an Organ Week. They both brought their own electronic organs from home and held three evenings of entertainment in a single week. The artistes booked were local boy Anthony Causier, (then in his teens), for a "popular" night, Michael Campbell (music master at Worcester College for the Blind) for a "classical" night and legendary cinema organist John Bee who wound up proceedings on the Friday with a Grande Finale Night. Since then most of the country's leading organists have made the journey to Whittington, including Ernest Broadbent from the Tower Ballroom Blackpool, Douglas Reeve from The Dome Brighton and Nigel Ogden a regular broadcaster on BBC's The Organist Entertains.

The group is organised by Debbie and Stan Slocombe, John Archer and a small band of volunteers who happily share responsibility for the eight Monday night concerts run each year. The admission prices of around £5 charged today are a far cry from the 20p to 35p charged in 1974!

Robert Wolfe provides the entertainment at the 1983 Christmas organ concert (BH)

Whittington Pre School Playgroup was formed in 1985 by Mrs. Jacqui Brown and Mrs. Sheila Cuddy, with the Village Hall providing an ideal rural setting. Following the departure of Mrs. Cuddy, Mrs. Gill Bampfield assisted Mrs. Brown with Mrs. Elaine Robertson and Mrs. Marion Wiltshire taking over from them. The playgroup has continued to feed the village school, and in line with current legislation has passed two 'Ofsted' inspections by the Office for Standards in Education. The group, which meets every weekday morning during term time, is now supervised by Mrs. Sharon Nash and remains a valuable asset for both the Village Hall and the community.

The Village Hall also presents a range of regular weekly activities. Whist drives take place most Mondays and Fridays; English country dancing takes place on Tuesday afternoons with ballroom and sequence dancing on a Thursday evening. Bingo sessions are held on a Wednesday evening, with the hall available at weekends for other local activities, jumble sales, craft fairs, private bookings etc.

All this is provided for the local community by a band of dedicated people from the local community.

THE CROOKBARROWERS

The Crookbarrowers organised dances, jumble sales and regular whist drives. The group was led by Horace Gammon, who was ably assisted by Joan Johns, Bunty Taylor, John Wilkes, Louis Huband and Bill and Iris Evans. A great deal of help was also received from Mr. and Mrs. Albert Wilkes of Highlands and Mr. and Mrs. R.A. Constance of Brean.

The profits from the events went either to local charities or towards providing entertainment for older people in the parish. Two half-day coach trips were organised annually; usually mystery trips, always providing a lavish tea for the pensioners. In addition, the Crookbarrowers laid on an annual evening supper with entertainment. When Richard Fletcher was headmaster of the College for the Blind (1959-1980) these suppers were held during the pupils' holidays using the College kitchens and dining hall. More latterly the senior residents' parties were held at the Village Hall, with around a hundred guests.

On special occasions, the Crookbarrowers sprung into action, for the Queen's Silver Jubilee in June 1977 they provided a cooked lunch for the pensioners of the village, in the Village Hall which was decorated in patriotic red, white and blue.

Following the deaths of John Wilkes, Joan Johns and Bill Evans, the remaining Crookbarrowers, who themselves were getting no younger, decided to bring their activities to a close. They should be remembered for the happy times they provided for many members of Whittington Village.

M5 MOTORWAY

The Ministry of Transport planned Britain's motorways and paid half the cost; the County Councils involved supervised the contractors and met the other half of the costs. No Government planning had ever before had such nationwide powers of compulsory purchase with every landowners objections being heard by a Ministry Tribunal.

The M5 from Exeter to Birmingham involved five County Councils; Devon, Somerset, Gloucester, Worcester and Warwick. The Worcestershire 'Twyning to Lydiate Ash' Section was the first to be started, the first to be completed, and the first to become out of date. It was built with only two lane carriageways, experience soon showed that three lanes were needed and elsewhere this was subsequently done.

A. Monk was the name of Worcestershire's contractors and Whittington became the headquarters of their operations. In 1958 the firm bought the three acres of Whittington Lodge from Mr. W.F. Spreckley. They occupied the house and erected two large sheds in the garden; professional calculations and figures smothered the inside walls. Monk's workforce gradually adopted the Village, and in 1961 threw the schoolchildren a wonderful Christmas party.

Whittington occupied an important site at the intersection of the M5 with the A44 Worcester to London road. At this point the A44 was then no more than 20 feet wide, and obviously unable to cope with the increase in traffic. The solution was to construct a dual carriageway between the motorway and a new roundabout at Red Hill. Since there was no room in front of The Swan, the road was routed on 'green' land behind it and crossed the motorway on a bridge with a roundabout on each side. This turned the 'old' A44 into a cul de sac and considerably shortened the long elm tree lined drive of Crookbarrow Farm. Consequently the Berkeley's lost land at Crookbarrow and Mr. March lost land at Chapelry Farm, both entered objections to the compulsory purchase. Whittington Parish Council objected also, as the safety of blind children crossing the new dual carriageway was paramount. The contractors met this objection by building a footbridge from inside the college grounds to the far side of the road.

On July 20th 1962 the Worcestershire section of the M5 was formally opened by Ernest Marples, the Minister of Transport. A motorcade formed up at the Southernmost point below Strensham, it travelled northward to the Worcestershire boundary at Lydiate Ash. There a ceremonial ribbon was cut and the road declared open. The motorcade then travelled back to Whittington and A. Monk at Whittington Lodge entertained the representative gathering.

By 1991 the Strensham (Junction 8) to Warndon (Junction 6) section was the only two lane stretch of the M5 between Exeter and Birmingham. With almost ¾ million vehicles per week using the M5 massive delays were a regular occurrence particularly during the peak hours or holiday periods.

This section of motorway was to be improved by the "Parallel Widening" method, which involved building a new three-lane carriageway and hard shoulder alongside the existing motorway. When the new carriageway was opened to traffic in one direction the existing motorway was modified to provide the other three lane carriageway and hard shoulder. This widening scheme also required the re-building of the Church Lane underpass and the demolition and re-building of the A44 road bridge and the bridge at Church Farm. Both bridges were quite literally blown up; the demolition of the A44 bridge saw hundreds of spectators crowded onto the Tump for a grandstand view. The Church Farm bridge was demolished on the evening of Saturday February 15th 1992, again watched by an audience of villagers.

The M5 was formally opened as a three-lane dual carriageway motorway on October 15th 1993. Only then did it become apparent that with more traffic travelling faster most of the Village had to contend with, at times, extreme levels of traffic noise. Protracted arguments by parishioners, the Parish Council and the local M.P. with the Highways Agency have still not managed to gain any substantial protection from the constant sound of high speed traffic.

Construction of the dual carriageway A44 passing behind The Swan Inn (WRO)

Construction work commences on the M5 Motorway. Looking South from what is now Junction 7 (BN/SP)

An early 1990's view of M5 Junction 7 prior to widening (HPJ)

Junction 7 during widening works (HPJ)

New junction and bridges being constructed around existing bridge (HPJ)

Old bridge has been demolished (HPJ)

Motorway widening and new Junction completed (HPJ)

AND FINALLY .....

Ted Hartwright, who has been associated with Whittington for all of his 90 years, was born at The Chapelry and has many memories of the village.

Ted recalls a gentleman named Tom Andrews who lived and farmed at Harkaway on the Pershore Road. Tom Andrews had been involved in fox hunting and it was he who named Harkaway after the hunting cry, he went on to write two books; 'Gin and Beer' and 'Horse, Hoof and Turf'.

Nearby, Woodhall was farmed by Mr. Hugh Kershaw in the 1920's. His horse 'Music Hall', a 9-year-old bay gelding, ran in the 1922 Grand National, winning it by 12 lengths. It is believed that Music Hall may have been fed on oats supplied by Ted's father, Mr. E. Hartwright Snr. from his business Holtham's in The Cornmarket, Worcester.

Continuing the connection with the horse, Ted remembers, as a young man, taking their own horses from The Chapelry up to The Forge for Arthur Johns to shoe them. This thriving blacksmith's business was later to become home to a well-known riding stables run by Arthur's daughter Joan. As well as giving riding lessons to local children, her pupils included blind boys from the College for the Blind. Her most famous customers were probably the singing trio, the Beverley Sisters, who in a recent local radio interview referred to their going horse riding in a small village near to Worcester.

Connie Hartwright, Ted's wife, who also grew up in Whittington, recalls Mrs. Green from Hill End giving parties for local children in the summer, on the lawns of her house.

Roy Rogers, also a resident of Whittington, remembers that during the war years, Mr. and Mrs. Green of Hill End allowed the school to use the cellars of their house as an air-raid shelter.

A hunt meeting at The Forge 1930's (RJ)

The Forge c1940 (RJ)

The Beverley Sisters pictured at The Forge (RJ)

102

Local children being entertained in the grounds of Hill End by Mr. and Mrs. Green (CTH)

A Whittington fete being opened by Lady Sumner in the 1920's (RJ)

A 1940's football match being played in the field next to Goldcliffe.
The roof of Birds House can be seen in the background. 1940's (BW)

Charlie Warner, pictured above, ran a smallholding in Church Lane, farming Little Red Field and Great Red Field. This area, very approximately ran from near to where the Village Hall now stands to Berkeley Close. He sold Great Red Field to Jack Tanner in 1954, having previously sold the other land incuding the piece on which the council houses in Berkeley Close were built, to Christopher March.

REFERENCES AND SOURCES

Benjamin Williams Leader R.A. 1831 - 1923; His Life and Paintings   Ruth Wood M.A.

Berrows Worcester Journal

Glossy Magazines Ltd. Oswestry

Kelly's Directories of Worcestershire

Littlebury's Directories of Worcestershire

St. Philip & St. James Church, Parish News

The College on the Ridge   Richard C. Fletcher

The Gables and its Tenants   John P. Correll

The Worcester Herald

The Worcestershire Hunt   Thomas Read Quarrell M.A.

Unseen Worcester, published by Parkbarn   Ray Jones

Whittington, Worcester The History of the Village (1977 and 1992)   M. Craze T.D., M.A.

Worcester Evening News

ACKNOWLEDGEMENTS

In producing this book I have received help and encouragement from many people, and would like to thank the following for their assistance in providing information and sourcing photographs etc.

Where the photographer is known their initials appear first, followed by letters indicating the source. Where the photographer is not known, only the source is shown. Occasionally the photographer and the source are the same.

ABM	Albert and Betty Morris	MEB	Midlands Electricity
AEW	Albert E. Wilkes	MT	Mick Tanner
AJ	Adrian Jones	P&S	Pitt & Sons
BH	Bruce Hodgkins	PG	Pam Goode
BN	Berrows Newspapers	PJ	Pat James
BPC	Braiswick Photographic Co.	PJW	Peter and Jannine Wheatley
BPS	Birmingham Post Studios	PM	Pat Mills
BW	Brian Wilkes	RBH	Rev. Bill Hopley
CS	Claire E. Siddall	RJ	Ron Jaynes
CSM	Colin and Sue Millington	RL	Rose Limrick
CTH	Connie and Ted Hartwright	RNIB	RNIB New College
DC	David Chestney	RP	Roger Phillips
EB	Eric and Eileen Bullock	RPJ	Rev. P. Jones
GM	Glossy Magazines Ltd.	RW	Ruth Wood
HC	Harold Coldicott	SK	Stan Kloock
HG	Horace Gammon	SP	Sid Painter
HPJ	Heather and Pete Jago	SSC	Scholastic Souvenir Co. Ltd.
I	Mrs Irving	TWH	The Worcestershire Hunt
IE	Iris Evans	UW	Unseen Worcester by Ray Jones
JA	Mr. and Mrs. J Appleton	W&DB	Wolverhampton & Dudley Breweries PLC
JB	Jennie Bruton	WCES	Whittington C of E Primary School
JL	Joan Limrick	WCL	Worcester City Library
JT	John Tanner	WP	William Preston
LH	Louis Huband	WRO	Worcestershire C.C. Record Office
LW	Les Wiltshire	WWH	W.W. Harris
MB	Maureen Butcher		

And to the countless others who have in any way helped with the compilation of this book.

Special thanks must also go to Carol Thompson who has typed and re-typed the drafts and spent a great deal of time helping with the research, selecting photographs and deciding on the final layout.